How to Start Your Own Small Business

Choosing the Right Business Structure

Scott Dion

Printed in the United States of America

First Printing, 2019

ISBN 978-1-7330910-0-8
Print Edition

Privacy Press
36 Center St., Suite 265
Wolfeboro, NH 03894
www.PrivacyPress.net

Table of Contents

Disclaimer

This book is not meant to be a replacement for proper advice from professionals in their respective fields. When and where appropriate, advice should be sought from accountants, CPAs, attorneys, and/or certain agents or agencies to safeguard against time, financial losses, or inadvertent error in the application of the law. Regulations and ordinances are continually changing, and various jurisdictions and venues have differing and sometimes contradictory applications of the law.

Although this book seeks to provide accurate information, it must be recognized that it was written at a particular point in time and addresses a general audience. Therefore, changes of law and situation may not be appropriate for a specific circumstance, and wisdom should dictate seeking additional advice and counsel for your individual needs.

The author, publisher, and editors are not liable for the use or misuse or the application of any of the ideas or information put forth herein. It is the responsibility of anyone who desires to utilize any of the information contained in this book to seek further advice on applying said information for their specific purposes.

Introduction

For over 30 years, I have been a business owner and entrepreneur. I have owned multiple businesses, partnered in others, and been on the board of yet others. The experiences I have gained from these companies, along with numerous businesses for which I have been an accountant and tax preparer, have given me a good understanding of common issues and concerns of many different types of firms. When I say types, I speak not only of machine, landscape, construction and employment companies, doctors' offices, consulting firms, and trucking companies but also of Sole Proprietorships, Partnerships, LLCs, Corporations, and Trusts.

Over the years of sitting down with people to do business and Estate Planning and to aid them in starting or reorganizing their own small businesses, I have been asked by many where I received all of my information. I suggest particular books or readings, such as those on Corporations or other specific subjects. People express that they are not so intent on one specific focus but on the broader scope, such as what I have portrayed to them in the previous hour or so of our meeting. When I go on to explain that I am at a loss to give them any one source or reference, they inevitably suggest that I should write such a book myself.

As a result of the many suggestions that have been made

over many years, I decided to attempt to write a book. I have been a licensed insurance agent and investment adviser, commodity trader, funds manager, and Real Estate broker and could fill a book on any one of those topics. However, numerous good sources can be found on each of those subjects.

Yet in my business of accounting, tax preparation, and business law consulting, I find people in general and small business owners in particular unwilling to delve too deeply into any of these topics, each of which can be very complicated and require a lot of time to become proficient in. Indeed, colleges offer degree-granting programs at a high cost to train the professionals licensed in these fields. Each of these fields and professions, just like that of medicine, is both general and specialized. For instance, you would not go to a brain surgeon for the flu or a cold nor go to a general practitioner for a brain tumor. Unfortunately, because of their lack of knowledge regarding the basics of business-related topics, many people seek out and overpay general practitioners for specialized service and vice versa, paying a high-priced specialist for a general need.

Therefore, this book is an attempt to help de-mystify certain topics and provide generalized knowledge to the small business owner or prospect. It is not meant to train anyone in accounting, tax preparation, or business law but rather to provide business owners with the tools needed to understand the various options available. This can make him or her better-equipped to both choose and direct the professionals, if any, who they hire. Having a greater understanding of certain concepts and options will aid business owners in more accurately expressing their goals and plans. This knowledge will enable them to be active participants in seeing those goals accomplished rather than be passive onlookers hoping they are paying for services that are actually in their best interest.

I ask in advance, and apologize up front, to all those readers who like their authors to be gender-neutral and who cringe at the constant use of "he" or even "she" as opposed to the words "person," "them," or any of the new politically correct methods of relaying the same information. Due to some of the concepts and ideas that I at times will try to convey, I feel that being sensitive and politically correct may make certain definitions and ideas all the more difficult to explain. Therefore, please accept that I am fully aware that women are every bit a part of today's business world as men—and have been a part of the small and family business scene long before it became vogue to recognize them for it. However, for simplification of ideas and shortening of sentences, I will not continually write "he or she." When I write one, you can infer the other. If I give the example of a father passing his business on to his sons, you can substitute these with mother and daughters.

That being said, I hope you will find tools and ideas within these pages that are beneficial. Whether you are thinking of going into business for yourself or have been doing so for years, I hope you will come away with ideas that will increase your profits, save you headaches, and benefit the lives of you and your loved ones.

CHAPTER 1

Getting Started

The best way to get started in anything is usually at the beginning, But since one of the main points of this book is providing the information that will help you make wise decisions, it will be necessary to put off the question of: "What type of entity should I start?" After making our way through the description of the many options available to you and the various advantages and disadvantages of each, we will then come full circle to the beginning: deciding if you will run your business as a "Sole Proprietorship," "Partnership," "LLC," "Corporation," or another form of business entity. Or maybe even some combination of these.

You may already be leaning toward a specific type because of some previous experience or comfort level, or perhaps because of things you have heard or the opinion of someone you know. It is my suggestion that you reserve making that decision and maintain an open mind as we examine the negative and positives of each type. It is not only the general advantages and disadvantages of these business types that should factor into your decision but also the way they fit into your specific goals.

What you are looking to accomplish and the nature of the business you are planning to run will be a big factor in making these decisions. So, what may have worked wonderfully for someone you know may not be the best move for you if indeed your objectives are different. My goal is to help make you confident in your ability to make choices that affect you. This is not to say that the advice you seek from others is not important; it most certainly is. But being able to better articulate to others just what advice you seek, without having to abandon the things you know and have already decided on, is a significant advantage. No one is or will be more interested in your success than you. Being able to blame someone else for your failure is no real consolation. Ultimately in business, the buck stops with you. Loss because of lousy advice or decision making is going to be felt, experienced, and carried by you, so take responsibility now right up front. Make your own decisions! Advice, counsel, and advisers are to be sought and weighed and used to make your own choices.

After an entity type is chosen, you will need to pick a name for it. You may already have something in mind, or you may need to brainstorm with others or sleep and meditate on it. For many, this is a crucial creative task that carries much significance. Some want a business with their own name. Others just want to relay the simple purpose or service such as Acme Roofing or Ace Plumbing. However you arrive at a decision, some of the things you need to know include the fact that any name other than your own is considered a fictitious name. Fictitious names in most jurisdictions require some type of registration. Depending on which state you live or are doing business in, registration may be done at the town, county, or state level.

In many cases, where you register will depend on the type

of entity. For instance, Jane Doe doing business as (dba), say "Creative Designs," a Sole Proprietorship, may require going down to her local town hall, fill out a one-page form, and pay a small fee to register her fictitious business name. This is done to protect the consumer. If anyone has a problem with "Creative Designs" and its products or services, they will have the means to find out that Jane Doe at some particular legal address is the responsible party.

For statutory entities such as a Limited Partnership, LLC, or Corporation, this registration process and application, which comes with somewhat higher fees, is done at the Secretary of State's (SOS's) office in your particular state. The need to register at the local level becomes unnecessary. For instance, submitting an "Application for Incorporation" along with "Articles of Incorporation" with the appropriate fees by Jane Doe for "Creative Designs, Inc." would accomplish both incorporation and name registration at all levels.

A trip to the SOS is certainly fine, but in most cases today is not necessary. Most states have online websites from which you can download all the needed forms, as well as directions and information about fees, that you can fill out and mail in, if not submit online. Many companies offer online services that will do it all for you for a fee. It should be mentioned here that in most cases, this quick registration will not include the actual legal contracts such as Partnership and LLC agreements between and for the parties involved. Although a Corporate Book and Stamp with several boilerplate agreements can be purchased relatively inexpensively online, they may not be the best and most complete method. More on this in another chapter.

Returning to the topic of the name itself, it may be wise to have ready a second or third choice in case your first is already being used; the state will not register two businesses of the same name. It may also be wise to do an Internet search to be sure that even if the name is available in your particular state, no well-known larger company of the same name exists elsewhere. Also checking for the availability of the name or a close match that you can be happy with regarding a .com, a .biz, or a similar domain address for a website is also a consideration in today's business world.

Most SOS's offices have an existing company search database you can check your prospective name against. If the name comes up it usually means it is already taken. If it cannot be found, then you can probably get the name for yourself. In many cases, you can pay a small fee to reserve an available name even if you are not quite ready to incorporate. If it's a favorite name, you may want to consider this along with your .com or other Internet registration as well.

The closeness of your name to another name can be more or less restrictive. Some states may allow "Creative Designs, Inc." For instance, if "Creative Product Designs" already exists, others may claim it is too close. That is why applying with a second choice attached may save you time. Otherwise, a rejection may be returned by mail, and you will need to apply again. Therefore, I suggest you do not order printed materials or other services before assurance that the name is yours.

Most states will not allow certain unlicensed business types to use deceptive or restricted names. For instance, you cannot make your Corporation appear to be a bank, Trust, Financial Company, etc. if you are not chartered as one. The state will not approve names that make you appear to be a state or federal agency when you are not. Federal Express, for instance, would not be a name you could get in this day and age. The same would apply if appearing to be an insurance company or public utility. In most cases, Corporations need to be designated as such by the use of "Incorporated," "Inc.," "Corporation," "Corp.," "Limited," "Ltd.," and "LLC or LP" for those entity types. Some techniques for attempting to get a name you like is to differ it slightly with designations such as "Associates," "Enterprises," "Group," etc. For example, although "Northeast Corp." may be taken you might instead try "Northeast Enterprises, Inc." or "Northeast Associates, Ltd."

Lastly, on the name issue, is consideration of your future goals and plans. Do you want a name that specifically pinpoints your current product or service? Or do you want it to be more nebulous, leaving room to branch out or change its primary focus, service, or product? A company called "Metal Roofing," for instance, nails the idea of attracting a customer looking for a metal roof, so if that is the business you are in, great! But what if you also do A-Frames, tar flat roofs on commercial buildings, and repair leaky shingle roofs? You will most likely lose prospects because of uncertainty about whether to contact you about anything other than a metal roof. In that instance, you may want to choose a name that is more all-encompassing or inclusive.

Some businesses provide a wide range of goods or services or rely heavily on word of mouth and reputation and do not want to be branded by a singular idea. They may go to the other extreme and pick a company name that doesn't pinpoint any particular product or service. Names such as "Rosebrook

Associates" or "Mid-West Enterprises" prevents anyone other than actual customers or clients from defining you or placing you in a particular mold. For those who want the best of both worlds, there is the reminder that not only individuals such as Jane Doe doing business as (dba) "Creative Designs" can use fictitious names. Like an individual, a generically named company such as "Mid-West Enterprises" can also do business as "Metal Roofing Co.," "Acme Trucking," or "Widget Sales Co."—or all of them at the same time. The customers of "Metal Roofing Co." may know nothing of "Acme Trucking" and vice versa, and neither may even know about "Mid-West Enterprises." Yet the employees of all of them may receive a check and benefits under "Mid-West." This same theme could be played out by a Corporation that owns several separate single-person LLCs, but let us hold off on those ideas until a later chapter.

After deciding on an entity and picking a name, you will need to choose an address or addresses. The application for registration, drawing up of contracts, and opening bank accounts, to name a few, will require the business address. Be mindful that many businesses have more than one address. Some have a main office or headquarters in one place and other offices, warehouses, and sales offices in other locations. Some start their small business in their home or garage or even the corner of the dining room table. With today's Internet and various technologies, cell phones, voice-over IP, UPS, and FedEx, two men and a truck who started their business last month can appear to be a major conglomerate the next. In my opinion, it is best to separate the privacy of your home and family life from that of business. That is not to say that having a small company in which you work from home is not to be desired.

On the contrary, many people very much desire that very thing. My suggestion is to consider a private mailbox (PMB) like "The UPS Store" or "Postal USA." Even the U.S. Postal Service today offers use of their physical street address along with a mail receptacle and a PO Box at the post office, and at the UPS Store a box that can be designated Suite #123. They both allow for physical receipt of packages from UPS and FedEx and regular mail all in one location.

Even if you later grow out of your home to an actual physical location elsewhere, you can either migrate your mail, packages, and literature to reflect the new office location or continue with the convenient and consistent addressing of the PMB or postal address established at the beginning. A business starting at an actual commercial address may still opt for the separate mailing address for its receivable, payable, and tax agency correspondences.

A mail-only address such as a PO Box alone will not serve all your needs. When given a PO Box, most tax agencies, banks, and others will request and even require a physical address as well, so it is better to already have it prepared to give. Remember that today's computers store everything forever, and that information becomes available to way too many people for comfort when it comes to certain private and personal matters. So, think ahead and tell computers only what you want them to know! Be aware that almost all businesses today have software for accounting and customer data that includes provisions for keeping track of multiple addresses. For instance, if you buy gifts from Walmart or Amazon.com, you can also list a name and address for each gift recipient to be shipped to separately directly from the store. In other words, their database keeps track of you—the customer—and several shipping addresses under the same account. So, bear these things in mind and use them for your convenience. For instance, the electric bill for your 123 Main St. office can be sent to "My Business Headquarters," 240 Industrial Park Road or elsewhere. "Mid-West Industries, Inc." may order and receive the bill for sheets of aluminum yet have them drop-shipped to its "Metal Roofing" business warehouse. Be aware, however, that these same conveniences may in other instances reveal relationships that you prefer do not exist or, should I say, are not known to exist.

Another topic that is somewhat related to the address issue is the consideration of a "Resident Agent." For a business conducted within your home state, serving as your own Resident Agent is normal and common. You could if you so desired still use your attorney, accountant, or another person who resides within your state. However, when considering registering and incorporating a business in a state in which you do not reside, you will need a Registered Agent who resides in that state. The reasons for considering incorporation in a state other than the one you reside in will be addressed in another chapter. For our current purposes, a Resident Agent is a person listed on the State Registration as someone who can be contacted or served legal process if the need should arise. For instance, if a consumer has a complaint or lawsuit he wants to bring against "Metal Roofing" of Delaware and the owner of "Metal Roofing" of Delaware lives in Maine, the person with the complaint is not required to find the owner in Maine to be able to bring his claim. If he has no other information, the SOS's office in Delaware will provide the name of the resident agent who, upon receiving the complaint, will be responsible for forwarding it to the owner in Maine. Whether or not the owner in Maine acknowledges receipt or actually does or does not receive it, the courts of Delaware will nonetheless consider the owner to have been served. Should the owner in Maine fail to maintain a Resident Agent in Delaware, the complaint served on the SOS's office will suffice to accomplish the same.

The Resident Agent, who is not an owner, does not have any liability for the business actions and is not the party being sued. He is only responsible for forwarding the complaint, notice, or legal service on to the proper party. It is the company that is responsible for being sure that the Resident Agent is aware of who and where that is, and that copies of said information are in the Resident Agent's hands should the state request it. In fact, many companies provide the very service of being a Resident Agent for other companies as a business in and of itself. Their fees range anywhere from $50 to $200 per year for this service, and they cover all 50 states.

Once you have submitted your name request along with registration forms and fees to the state, you will receive a stamped copy back with a number that identifies your entity to that office. At this point, you are assured that the name is yours to use and do business with.

After taking the previous steps, you should obtain an EIN / TIN for your business from the Internal Revenue Service (IRS). The initials EIN and TIN stand for either "Employer Identification Number" or "Tax Identification Number"; they are the same number and the terms are used interchangeably. Not all businesses immediately have employees, hence the term "Tax Identification Number." If and when you do have employees, they will be referred to by an "Employer Identification Number." On various forms and at different times, one or the other may be referred to but it is this same nine-digit number that you will use.

With today's Internet access, this is about a 15-minute process online. Although you can still mail it in or fax an application for EIN / TIN, the most practical way is to go online and go through the form, answering various questions about name, address, start dates, etc. When you finish, choose the option to print out your number and IRS letter. I suggest you print to a computer file and save a copy to Adobe Acrobat or in a similar format. This way you can retrieve the file whenever you need a printed copy.

When completing the application online, you will come across a question asking if or how many employees you estimate you will have in the first 12 months. Even if you are planning to hire right away, I suggest you answer "none." Not doing so sets up a certain expectancy that, if not met, will cause the IRS to send out requests for missing reports, etc. Correcting IRS errors can prove very frustrating and therefore I suggest waiting until there is an actual payroll. Additionally, if you use a payroll service or an accountant, they may have their own submission methods and system, and there will be no need for the printed materials and coupon booklets from the IRS.

After you obtain an EIN / TIN number, your attorney or accountant—if you are using said advisers—will want to check on any other necessary tax registrations. These may include state or federal requirements concerning tax deposits and other reports regarding such things as income, sales, meals, or use taxes depending on the type and nature of your business, product, or service. Again, the SOS's office in each state will have a host of information on these issues, most of it online today.

Now, with a copy of your Entity Registration stamped by the state and a copy of your IRS EIN / TIN number and letter, you are ready to go down to your local bank or credit union and open a business account. For many, a single checking account may suffice, but the addition of an attached savings account or additional checking account may be warranted in some cases. Keeping a General Account and a Payroll Account separate is one consideration. Another factor—depending on the business type—is holding client funds such as deposits, retainers, and escrow funds separate from the General Account until such funds are earned and invoiced. In some cases, this may be a requirement.

Most business accounts today come with debit cards and online account access. If, when opening an account, they are not mentioned you should inquire about them. Being able to check deposits and debits in real time can be a great convenience. Also, the ability to transfer amounts from checking to savings or from the General Account to the Payroll Account is convenient. By using debit cards for point-of-sale items such as fuel, supplies, and on-the-road meals, which are deductible as business expenses, you can avoid the more cumbersome method of keeping track of petty-cash and cash-slip reimbursement for out-of-pocket expenses.

Signatories for accounts need to be considered with an eye on both convenience and security. Some business owners may insist on being the only signatory or debit cardholder. The drawback to this, depending on the type of business and its daily functions, is that if the owner is not present, an emergency payment, a COD delivery, or a needed supply order cannot be made without you being there. Although adding your secretary, office manager, or another responsible party as a signatory may solve these problems, finding out later that they were untrustworthy can lead to heartache and financial loss. A method of balancing such concerns may be the issuing of debit cards or credit cards with various maximums per purchase or per day. Individual check-signing for amounts up to specific values can be approved, and anything exceeding the chosen limit would require two signatures.

Setting up a merchant account either with your bank or an online provider is another consideration. The easier it is for a customer to choose to do business with you the more likely the sale. If I have to pay for your services today out of my currently available cash, I may be reluctant or forgo the purchase for another time. But if I can have it now and pay later, I am much more readily convinced. Now, this may not be a great personal habit to live by, but it is the reality of too many in today's economy. Unfortunately, given a choice to spend what's in their pocket or pay another day with someone else, most people will choose to pay later.

Merchant accounts do shave off a couple of percentages of each dollar for the Banker, so the desire for immediate business and pricing models needs to be weighed. In the long run, the fees for a merchant account are preferable to the losses that can occur from either not offering the option or extending too much credit yourself with Open Accounts.

Now that you have a registered business with tax numbers and bank accounts, you are ready to receive income, loans, and investments, and pay for goods, supplies, and services—the expenses of your own business. It is crucial that you keep track of every dime in and out from this point on. The better job you do, the more you are going to save in payments to accountants, lawyers, and tax agencies in the long run. Do not forget to log in the amounts you spent on the registration fees, Internet fees, and so forth; these are all start-up costs to be expensed.

There are many good bookkeeping software packages out there today. Software such as One Write, Peachtree (now Sage 50cloud), and QuickBooks makes keeping track of all financial transactions very easy. My favorite is QuickBooks. It's as simple as writing checks or deposit slips and, by using your computer and printing them out, all transactions are logged at the same time. Today's versions can even check your bank and credit card balances and be used as your merchant account provider as well. This, along with as little as five folders for physical records, will keep you organized enough for an accountant to do your year-end tax returns.

Label one of the five folders "Receivables"; it will hold all your copies of invoices to your customers. The second folder should be marked "Paid Receivables"; it will hold all the copies from folder one after the customer has paid them. Label the third folder "Bills" or "Payables," for the bills your company needs to pay. Mark the fourth folder "Receipts," for the bills in folder three after you pay them, and jot down the check number used. In the fifth folder, put your copy of the business registration, IRS's EIN number and letter, any other contracts, insurance policies, etc., and mark it "Legal." This simple five-folder system will get most small businesses through their first year with or without computer software. I do recommend the

QuickBooks Pro from the get-go if possible.

Depending on the type of business, a physical folder system may need to be expanded. But for the most part, it will be an expansion of that very system. You may require a folder, however, for each customer under the "Receivable" category and a folder for each vendor under the "Bills" category such as electric, phone, disposal, etc., but that is the general idea.

You are ready to transact business and keep track of the transactions. Most companies not only provide a product or service but need products and services themselves. They may need to lease a location from which to do business. This leads to the need for phone service, electric service, heat, landscaping, trash removal, raw materials from which to make their products, and the list goes on.

These services and products should be purchased and contracted for by the business itself and not in the name of the owner or Partners individually. It is true that the company may not have any credit of its own at first. Should security, credit, or guarantees need to be made, the owner's name, credit, and guarantee may be requested. In such cases, it is still preferable to contract services in the name of the business; the owner can always sign personally for surety if need be. By being a guarantor, the service provider can be assured of payment by the credit of the individual. But for the sake of building credit for the business and properly assigning income and expenses to the company, the transactions are done in the business name. That way there will be no need for confusion or argument with the IRS or others as to ownership of property, income, and expenses. For instance, if a cell phone, vehicle, or other item or service is in an individual's name and the company makes the payment, the question can arise, "Is the company paying the individual's bill?" Is it for a business purpose? Is it 100% business or part business and part personal? Is it compensation, fringe benefit, or for the sake of the business not having its own credit? However, if the same good or service is in the company's name, it is simply the company paying its own bill, its own expense! Nothing to explain, end of story.

Phone services, web addresses, and emails should be considered carefully. These methods of communication and contact go into databases kept by others and are the means of reaching you to contract business. Therefore, a customer's ease in remembering your company and its long-term use and availability are important. If I do business with you this year and then need you again in a year or two, my first attempt to reach you will be by the same phone number, email, or web address. If these do not remain the same, my effort to relocate or contact you may get sidetracked and I may turn to a competitor during my search. Voice over IP and 800 number services may be considered. These services usually have fancy options for forwarding to cell phones and other business lines or automatically following a list of optional numbers to forward to by priority and sequence. These options make it possible to field live calls from any location. They can be directed to whoever is currently providing coverage in your company whether they are here or there. These features allow you to have a real person answering your business number a higher percentage of the time. Nothing will separate you from your competition like availability. When someone calls a business, they want to reach a person, not an answering machine. Even if they can't speak to you or the person they seek, they want to know the message was received. Electronic gadgets and computers are great tools, but people do business with people. They give their business to people they like. The attitude and attentiveness of those who answer your business lines are every bit as important as that of the professional doctors, engineers, scientists or whatever skilled or knowledgeable person they are trying to reach.

A related consideration is marketing—signs, advertisements, and listings. Years ago, getting into the yellow pages, putting a sign out front, and maybe running a local newspaper ad were options for promoting the small local business. Today there is the Internet, cable TV, radio, Google, Ad Words, websites, and way too many others to list. It is not the purview of this book to explore these options. Many such sources exist and finding them is not a bad idea for any business owner. I will speak here only to a couple of points related to getting started and business law. Before you run out and get a 30-foot high neon sign to stick out in front of your business, be sure to check the local ordinances, bylaws, and zoning rules to find out what the law is regarding such things as height, size, and illumination restrictions. You don't want to be paying big money for signs only to get a visit from the code enforcement officer in your town telling you it needs to come down.

Similarly, many companies develop logos, mission statements, and taglines to put on signs and literature. Before you put yours into use be sure to do a comprehensive and hard search to be sure you are not considered to be copying someone else's copyright, trademark, or patent. Again, receiving a letter from the attorneys of a much larger company demanding that you cease and desist can be time-consuming and potentially expensive. Likewise, if you have created, invented, or designed something unique, you may also want to protect it. Although you can claim a common law trademark (TM) or copyright (C), you may want to go the extra step and apply to the U.S. Patent and Trademark Office for a registered trademark or patent. Certain fees and documents need to be submitted, and that also by itself is the subject for a whole other book.

In the meantime, before incurring such an expense, certain poor-man's steps can be taken to document and witness the date and fact of your invention, trademark, or writing. For instance, packaging your written materials and mailing them to yourself and/or a witness will employ the U.S. Postal Service as a witness through their date and time stamp. Be sure to leave the package unopened against a future opening in a court of law, if necessary. Other steps can involve witnesses and notaries and sending copies to your attorney, etc. I include the subject here only to make you aware that such issues exist.

A couple more items I think every business should consider and have ready are, first, a "Credit Sheet" to give out to vendors (people and businesses you are getting goods and services from), and second, a 'Payment Options Sheet" or package to hand out to your customers.

Your company name and logo should appear at the top of the Credit Sheet, which should also include pertinent information usually requested on applications for a loan or credit line. Also listed should be the company address, a list of its owners or officers, phone and fax numbers, and email addresses followed by names and addresses of other companies that you do business with and that extend credit to you. The Credit Sheet should list banks and credit card companies and their contact numbers, and even a contact person's name who will hopefully say good things about you. Having this information ready in your own format will make you appear organized and professional and indicate that you indeed have other Open Accounts. This will save you much time in the long run because whenever you request an open account or credit line from another company they will usually send, fax, or email you an application. I have found this method to be much simpler than filling out all the various applications you may receive. Stamp your company name on the top of their application, in the body of it write "See Attached," and then attach your own pre-formatted Credit Sheet to it. I have never had complaints about using this method; occasionally you may be asked to sign the application near some legal paragraph expressing your agreement to pay within terms of the credit extension.

The term "Open Account" refers to the extension of credit by someone you purchase goods or services from that allows you a specific period of time in which to pay. For instance, a construction company may want the ability to call or stop in and pick up lumber and tools for a particular job they are doing without the need to make a payment each time their employee runs over to fill another need. The lumber yard has the pickup person sign that he received the lumber, and once a month the lumber yard lists the items and bills the construction company, which agrees to pay within 15 or 30 days or whatever terms are usual to that particular industry.

Having Open Accounts reduces the amount of upfront money you need to service your customer before collecting your money. Companies just starting out may not have many or even any Open Accounts. In this case, a good option is to use utility accounts or visiting vendors with whom you leave a deposit to create a secured open account. Then you would use these for your Credit Sheet. As you accumulate actual credit and larger vendors you can edit your Credit Sheet to reflect the changes. If you regularly do business with a supplier with whom you do not have an open account, use his desire to keep you as a customer by requesting that he give you some level of terms, even if very low to start, or ask how many times you will be required to make cash purchases before he will extend terms. If he continues to refuse, it may be a point you can use with any competitor of his that might want your account instead.

The other side of this coin is knowing how you are going to handle your customers and their requests for Open Accounts, terms, and credit. Depending on your business type and the industry standards, you may or may not need to deal with Open Accounts. But if you are in an industry where all your competitors offer such accounts, you may need to manage such a system yourself. For instance, regarding the other side of the issue, illustrated in the previous example of a lumber yard, you may prefer cash on the barrel. Who wouldn't? As a lumber yard owner, you may get the occasional homeowner to pay as they go, but many carpenters, contractors, and home builders will go elsewhere without payment terms. Therefore, I suggest that you also have a Credit Application for your customers that outlines your terms and requirements for opening an account. It should request all the information you require to make a decision about whether or not a particular customer qualifies and for how much. The "how much" obviously will also be determined by your own company's size and ability to extend credit.

Along with this, you should have a simple one page "Payment Options Sheet" that has your company's letterhead with address, telephone, email, etc., along with a list of methods such as cash, check, Master Card / Visa with a box for adding that information and a signature. It can also include any bank wire transfer or Swift Code information for payment from bank to bank with, of course, a mention at the bottom regarding Open Account applications being available (see Appendix D).

CHAPTER 2

Other Considerations

Several considerations will go into deciding the best business entity or structure to use. The general advantages and disadvantages of each—Sole Proprietor/dba, General Partnership, Limited Partnership, LLP, LLC, Corporation, Trust, Association, or Non-Profit—will depend largely on your goals and objectives. A few others may include the availability of or need for start-up funds and other capital, business type, jurisdiction, and taxation issues.

For instance, do you have the capital or savings to fund your own business? How much money will be required to get the business up and running before its income from goods or services will be sufficient to provide for itself and begin generating a profit? If you do not have the needed capital, are you planning to borrow the funds, or are you taking on a partner or maybe offering an interest in your business in exchange for an investment? Will this borrowing or investing be done with Bankers, Angel Investors, Partners, friends, or family?

Although they are usually the least expensive, bank funds can be the most difficult to secure. No matter how many TV commercials you see produced by certain big-name banks befriending the small local businessman and aiding him in becoming a thriving business, you will be hard-pressed to find a real-world example. For the most part, banks lend money to people who can prove they don't need it. In other words, if you have enough equity in your home or some other asset or income stream that they can attach a Lien to, then they may let you use it to raise funds for your business. Then they will Lien your business and the equitable property and require your personal guarantee. So if you have excellent credit and equity, then you can get liquid cash most cheaply from the bank and will not need Partners or investors. This will make all your business decisions entirely your own.

If you are not in this position or consider a Lien or the encumbering of your name and assets acquired elsewhere to be an unacceptable risk against a new venture, you may have to move on down the list. Relying on Partners may be a way of sharing the risk. This requires finding others who are excited about your idea, think it is sound, and would like to help a business get off the ground with limited risk by agreeing what each will contribute and receive if it is successful. This option will allow you to protect your home and any other property or business ventures from the risk factors associated with the new enterprise. The compromise, of course, may come with the need to meet the goals and objectives of others besides your own. There are endless stories, both horrific and wonderful, regarding the success of past Partnerships. They are not for everyone—and maybe not even for most. But in the coming pages, I hope to offer some methods of making these risks more manageable.

Angel investors are yet another avenue of raising capital. Like banks, these professional money investors and managers do not hand over money willy-nilly; their rates of interest are steeper, and the control and oversight they seek are usually firm and complete. Unlike a bank, they may not require your home or other assets and will consider the merits of the business idea or invention for which you are seeking funding. All of this is good. But a poorly crafted agreement on your part or the accepting of too high an interest rate may quickly make the business theirs rather than yours, and that obviously doesn't meet your goals.

Another consideration is the raising of capital from friends and family, whether by taking a loan or by giving them a limited, non-controlling interest such as a portion of stock in your newly formed corporation. The advantages are, of course, raising funds while still owning the lion's share of the business and maintaining complete control. The disadvantages are the shame involved with failing and losing their money should that occur. We all know that money can come between the good relations of families and friends. This is not to be taken lightly, as such heartache and turmoil can last years beyond the business venture. Another drawback to borrowing funds is that you would usually offer a payment plan and schedule, and the need to make these payments adds to the business expenses. The alternative, giving stock and part ownership interests, takes away the need to schedule payments and therefore is less burdensome for a business in its early stages. The downside is that this is essentially a profit-sharing venture; unlike a loan, investors risk never being paid back but instead share in profits forever. These both need to be weighed going in. Certainly, a piece of the pie is better than no pie at all—without the funds the pie would never be made.

Another consideration will be what type of business you are conducting. When I speak of what type of entity, I am talking about Partnership versus LLC versus Corporation and so on. But when I talk about business type, I am referring to what your business does. Is it a business that provides services like lawn mowing, roofing, or house painting? Or does it provide professional services such as accounting, legal, or medical? There are also manufacturing businesses that use raw materials to produce a finished product, and companies with further divisions between retail and wholesale. What makes up your business marketplace? Are your customers the general public or a specific segment? Are they other businesses? Business-to-consumer versus business-to-business may have a direct bearing on the type of entity or, in some cases, entities you will choose to establish. For instance, a company that deals directly with a large segment of the public may want to keep their physical inventory and assets at a minimum and be sure its owners and officers have limited liability. Due to the higher odds of a complaint or lawsuit, a company whose nature is to have many assets such as machinery or other property in order to provide its goods or services may consider having a company with little or no assets up front. This way the up-front company deals with the public and the high-asset company deals only with the up-front company, thereby reducing its direct exposure.

In conjunction with business type is the consideration of jurisdiction. Should the business be based in your home state or another state? This question involves a combination of several factors: not only business type but entity type, ownership structure, taxation issues, and your goals and objectives for the company's growth. A business with a vision for future growth, with sales in multiple states and jurisdictions, will seriously consider its initial registration or incorporation. Some states have laws very favorable to business while others are very burdensome.

Many Corporations are formed in business and tax-friendly states such as Delaware, Nevada, or Wyoming even though their majority stockholders/owners live elsewhere. These states charge no state income or sales taxes outside their state and a limited amount within it. This means, for instance, that a corporation in Wyoming can do business in every U.S. state and around the world and owe no income or sales tax. This leaves it with only a federal income tax requirement rather than both a federal and state income tax, as in many other states. A company incorporated in Massachusetts, for instance, would be at a competitive disadvantage to a Wyoming corporation performing the same services or selling the same product, considering that the former will have all its income taxed in addition to the federal rate.

The same consideration by the high-asset company and its up-front sales to the consumer company described previously would not only save some income taxes. It would also further insulate and protect the asset-rich company from its up-front sales company by splitting it into two separate jurisdictions. This would decrease the likelihood of a public consumer in, say, Massachusetts, filing suit against the up-front Massachusetts company and additionally trying to reach the asset-rich company in Wyoming that manufactured and sold the product to the Massachusetts sales company. This is because doing so would require the consumer to file suit in Wyoming since the company is not under Massachusetts jurisdiction. Further, the consumer did not actually transact any business with the manufacturer in Wyoming.

Now before anyone jumps on their high horse, I am not advocating consumer fraud or bad business practices. I am a firm believer that whenever possible, the old idea that the customer is always right should be adhered to. Any business-person who values their business, their reputation, and their word should bend over backward to settle any and every complaint and dissatisfaction. When anyone harms or damages another, he should do everything in his power to make it right, provide reimbursement, and correct the problem. That said, we all know that lawyers and the courts in this country along with excessive and burdensome government regulations are ruining this great nation and driving businesses out and under in droves. We also know that many unscrupulous individuals go around seeking situations or lawsuits that will make them rich. This book is about starting a business, staying in business, and protecting your business. Therefore, my examples will tend toward that view. There are plenty of consumer protection books and resources to be found, but that is not the focus of this book.

If someone sues your business for damages and your business structure prevents him from prevailing against you, great. But if you know you owe him, do what's right and pay him anyway. On the other hand, if someone's claim should be for $5,000 and they try to collect a million, shame on them and hurrah for you when they fail. You will be glad you didn't listen to the liberals frowning on asset protection.

CHAPTER 3

Sole Proprietor

The "Sole Proprietor" or "Sole Proprietorship" is one of the most common small-business types. Sole Proprietor basically means One Owner or Individual Owner. It is most often used or referred to along with the term "Doing Business As" or "dba," initials representing an individual doing business under a name other than their given name. For instance, Jane Doe, an individual owner or Sole Proprietor, may run a business that does custom designs of some particular item. Rather than naming her business Jane Doe's she may name it "doing business as" "Creative Designs." Therefore, technically her business is Jane Doe dba "Creative Designs," a Sole Proprietorship. The public will see the business as "Creative Designs" and give little thought as to what type of entity it is.

Although some people prefer using their own name for their individually owned business, the majority in this type of entity do business under an alternative name. This alternative name is also called a fictitious name. Most jurisdictions require people doing business in a name other than their own to pay a small fee and register the business. Depending on the state where you reside or are performing the business in, the registration may be done at your town hall, the county offices, or the SOS's office. The reason this is required is usually for consumer protection. If a customer, vendor, or other party has a problem or dispute with a fictitiously named business, their effort to confront the responsible party may be hampered if they cannot determine the owner or responsible party listed on the application, which is a public record.

Although many individuals do business in this type of entity, I believe it has much less to do with being favored and more to do with being the default for those who do not fully understand their options. Many Sole Proprietors begin their small business on the side, using the skills or ideas acquired from having worked a job and developed expertise or talent over some time. So understandably their focus is on providing their skills and not so much on accounting, taxes, entity, and Estate Planning.

The definite advantage of the Sole Proprietorship is the ease and speed at which you are off and running. The disadvantages, however, may develop over time in all the areas that have been mentioned. Lack of proper planning can cost you thousands in accounting, taxes, Estate Planning, and unprotected liabilities. What you don't know and didn't bother finding out can hurt you—a lot!

Sole Proprietors pay more taxes, experience more audits, and have more liability than any other group in the United States. They have full liability for all their actions, debts, and damages, both business and personal. Because you *are* your business, any personal liability owed will attach to you personally and extend to your company. You and your business are married. Your personal tax return and business tax return are married, as they are one and the same. Because your business return is filed for on a Schedule C along with your personal

1040 tax return, whether single or married filing joint, a problem with one is a problem with the other.

You have probably heard the saying, "Work smarter, not harder." Well, in today's business environment, you not only need to work smarter—you also need to *plan* smarter. In my opinion, the Sole Proprietorship should be among the least-used entities rather than the most. No matter how many hours or how much of your life is wrapped up in your business, you would be wise to separate your personal life and assets from your Business Assets. By separating assets and limiting your business liabilities, a business problem can remain a business problem and a personal problem a personal problem. Your personal tax return will be separate from your business return. And if you have more than one business, one business's problems can cause problems with another. If you are already a Sole Proprietor, don't despair; this is one of the easiest entities to convert to another type should you so choose.

Sole Proprietors, as well as the owners of interests in other types of entities (especially Partnerships and LLCs), often take profits and personal income from their businesses in various ways. Although any type of business can set up payroll and establish the usual employer-to-employee relationship with W-2 reports and withholding and include its owner, many do not. Many owners just withdraw funds here and there as needed. Depending on the entity type, this may cause some confusion between calculating earned income, dividends, or profit share at year-end. Be aware that the profits from your Sole Proprietorship will be considered your income at that time. Whether or not you have done tax withholding on yourself, your income tax return will compute the tax amounts due for Social Security and Medicare as well as the income tax amount. For self-employed persons, this includes the amount you would pay as an employer added to the amount you would pay as an employee. If not planned for, these amounts can be a surprise and leave you scrambling at year-end.

Additionally, after your first year in business, the IRS expects the self-employed individual who is not on a W-2 payroll plan to submit quarterly estimates. These reports and payment deposits are expected to come within 10% of your actual tax due at year-end. The amount outside that range will govern tax penalty amounts added. A rule of thumb is to take last year's tax due amount and round it up slightly, and then divide that figure into four equal payment deposits for the current year. So, if you owed just under $10,000 last year, you would make four $2,500 payment deposits this year. Again, this advice applies not only to Sole Proprietorships but to all self-employed individuals and holders of interests in Partnerships, LLC's, associations, and even Corporations, especially the S Corporation.

CHAPTER 4

General Partnership

The "General Partnership" is a business entity consisting of two or more persons getting together for a business purpose. It is probably one of the oldest forms of business and can be statutory or non-statutory. Depending on the activities undertaken and the relationship of the individuals concerning those activities, a Partnership may be considered to have been formed whether or not a formal written agreement has been entered into by those individuals.

All Partners in a General Partnership are considered general Partners and all have full liability for its actions and debts jointly and severally, even if they hold varying percentages of the total ownership. If a person does not intend this circumstance or has significant personal assets, such a relationship should be avoided. For this reason, few General Partnerships are purposely formed these days. Most people opt for the more popular business forms such as LLC, Corporation, or Limited Partnership.

Although in most jurisdictions registration is not required for a General Partnership, the registration of a fictitious name may be needed. Such registration may also prevent name duplication within your state. Due to the "Statute of Frauds," it is always advisable to put agreements in writing. Many problems and disagreements can be avoided by having shared expectations as well as defined responsibilities. The Statute of Frauds relieves the courts of the responsibility to hear and decide cases for the arguments of aggrieved parties when the dollar value exceeds the statutory amount, and the parties have failed to put their agreement terms in writing. Said amount may be as low as $500 in some venues.

One use and advantage of a simple General Partnership agreement in today's business environment would be to protect individuals working together on a joint venture from having one individual be considered the employee of another, thereby avoiding misunderstandings regarding employee tax withholding or Workman's Compensation Insurance.

The law in most states today provides that any business, whether a Sole Proprietor, LLC, Corporation, or General Partnership, needs to provide Workers Compensation Insurance starting at the moment employee number one is hired. This requirement is usually waived for company owners themselves, although the option usually exists to have it apply to the owners as well if so desired. At times this can be a good idea. This coverage compensates any worker who is injured on the job and will cover medical costs and a portion of lost wages.

For the purposes of this chapter, note that it makes a big difference if the person working next to you in your business is your employee or your partner or co-owner. Partners in a General Partnership, members of an LLC, and owners of other entity types are not usually required to have insurance for themselves, nor are they required to withhold taxes on each other as a W-2 employee.

Let's say self-employed carpenter Jack is doing business as "JC Builders" and receives a contract to build a barn for customer McDonald. Because it is a big job, Jack decides to have self-employed carpenter Stanley help him. Jack plans to pay Stanley a percentage or fixed portion of the amount being charged to McDonald. After agreeing on the dollars involved, they start the job. A few days in, Stanley falls from a ladder and is seriously injured. An ambulance takes Stanley to the hospital and conveys that an accident has occurred at work. The hospital assumes that he has Workers Compensation Insurance coverage and bills accordingly.

A week or two later, "JC Builders" receives a cease and desist order from a state employee, who tells Jack that the state has discovered that because he does not have Workers Compensation Insurance, his business must cease operations until he acquires it. Jack tries to explain that he has no employees and does not need that coverage. He is told to take the matter up at his upcoming hearing. Jack attends the hearing, sure he will straighten the whole thing out since he knows the law doesn't require him to have Workers Compensation Insurance when he has no employees. He plans to explain that Stanley worked for himself and was just a contractor. Upon arriving at the hearing, Jack sees Stanley's wife with a guy he doesn't know, and she seems like she's avoiding having a conversation. Suddenly the case is called, and the stranger with Stanley's wife steps forward and announces himself as an attorney representing the injured party who is still in the hospital. He explains how it has come to their attention that Mr. Stanley's employer, Jack of JC Builders, was conducting business without the legally required insurance.

Jack jumps up, appalled at the characterization, and explains that he is not an employer and that Stanley was a contractor who worked for himself at the time of the injury. The attorney interjects that this is not the family's understanding and that Stanley has suffered injury, is hospitalized, and has lost wages since the accident. After another round of outrage and stammering, Jack is asked if he is an attorney or has representation. When he replies that he does not, he is advised to hire one and a new hearing date is set. Jack returns home very upset, only to find his wife is also upset after having been visited by a very arrogant man from a Federal Agency called OSHA (the Occupational Safety & Hazard Administration).

Do you think this is a far-fetched, highly unlikely scenario? If you do, you would be very wrong. This situation and many very similar ones occur daily in the good ole' USA these days. I have personally aided clients in the settlement after the fact in three such situations over the past several years. Even the quickest and easiest settlements in such cases involve great expense, frustration, and anxiety for all. Hiring so-called "under the table" workers, self-employed individuals with no official business registration or partnering without agreements in place, should be avoided like the plague.

This situation could have been avoided by planning for proper insurance coverage and documented agreements. Even in industries where the use of contractors and subcontractors is the norm, having Contractor Agreements and even a one- or two-page Partnership agreement on temporary jobs and joint ventures can be lifesavers. Setting shared expectations and having an orderly and documented system of business-to-business transactions will establish a record and history of the legal and ethical manner in which you conduct your business. Preventing even one such scenario as the one described herein will be worth its price in gold.

As stated, although they are not widely used today, General Partnerships can have their place in business. Used properly and creatively they can save you money and headaches. Partnerships can be between two individuals or among many individuals. They can also be between one entity type and another or between multiple entities. Corporation A may be a business with its own products and marketplace. It can become Partners with Corporation B, which also has its own products or services that are totally independent of Corporation A. Yet if the two companies have a shared goal or product, they could become Partners in Partnership C in an effort to gain a share of a particular marketplace.

A Partnership does not have to denote a 50/50 ownership. Ownership interests can vary depending on the agreement of the parties. They can be 60/40, 70/30, or even 1/99%. Be aware that Partnerships with uneven interests, such as ownership interests of over 90% and others under 10%, may not be considered a bona-fide interest for some uses. For instance, for Worker's Compensation purposes, giving a person a 5% share in your Partnership may not cause him to be considered an owner rather than an employee, nor will it prevent the IRS's requirement to withhold from employees. Individual financial institutions may have similar issues. In other words, be careful of ideas that are ploys. The rule should be substance over form, not the other way around. Meaning it may not hold up just because it's on paper if it's not also the actual practice or the real deal!

CHAPTER 5

Limited Partnership

A "Limited Partnership" is the first of the statutory entities I will describe. A statute is a law enacted by a legislative body. "Statutory" technically means "imposed by statute." Sole Proprietorships, General Partnerships, and certain Trusts have statutes that apply to them. Therefore, they can be considered to be statutory, but they can also be considered non-statutory. This is because they are deemed to be of common right under the Common Law. Common Laws are legal practices and traditions based on long-held social custom and practices that have the same force as laws passed by legislative bodies. On the formation of the United States, the English Common Law was adopted and made a part of our legal system under the Constitution for the united States of America. Individual laws and ordinances would later be adopted and ratified by various legislative bodies to be formed in the several states. The Constitution is considered the law of the land. The Constitution, Article 1, section 10, states that the "Right to Contract" shall not be impaired. That being the case, all contracts between parties entered into knowingly, willingly, and for a lawful purpose are binding on the parties involved, and such rights and obligations should not be interfered with by the state or others. A contract into which one party is forced is no contract at all. Also, contracts that a person is tricked into entering or where all the terms are not disclosed upon entering are also not enforceable. There is a difference between the terms "legal" and "lawful." Yet the sophistry of the courts in recent years has made unlawful actions legal. So although lawful has long been held to be right and correct or righteous, legal refers to actions upheld and enforced in the courts.

In the United States, men and women are supposed to be free and therefore able to take any lawful action they desire without let, hindrance, or license. A man's labor is his property. Hence, he is free to take his property (labor) and combine it with another man's property (his labor). Together they can then sell that property or perform their labor together (a General Partnership) for yet another person (customer) in exchange for goods or property such as gold or silver (money). This arrangement would be an example of a non-statutory General Partnership; the General Partners are fully liable and responsible for their actions and debts. This is as it should be and lawful.

The "Limited Partnership," "LLC," "Corporation," and many types of "Trusts" are statutory entities and exist not because they are lawful but because they are legal. These entity types offer their owners, Partners, and stockholders what is called "limited liability." Limited liability means the men and women involved in these "legal" entities are not fully liable for their actions and debts. This would be unlawful and unrighteous if it were not made "legal" by the state. This is why you make application, register a fictitious name, and agree to pay taxes and fees in exchange for state protection against parties who could and would otherwise hold you fully liable for your word and actions. In other words, the state uses its power to make "legal" actions that are otherwise unlawful and unrighteous. The state is technically a protection racket. That is why state tax agencies and the IRS act like they are your Partners because, in fact, they are.

Today most people think that having a company with "Limited," "LTD," "Inc.," etc. after the company name makes it appear prominent or prestigious when in fact the law requiring such designations were put in place to be a warning to the public. The warning is a notice that lets you know you are not dealing with a fully responsible party but instead with someone you may never be able to reach to get satisfaction. It's a sign initially meant to say, buyer beware!

I know that this explanation is not very flattering to the nature of business today. Those few people with consciences still intact may be reluctant to participate at all in such a system. Unfortunately, it is the only one out there, and there is no other court system for business outside our system of legal fictions.

One of the reasons for my discussion regarding statutory entities is to touch upon the importance of your contracts, not only for a Limited Partnership but for any entity. Most states have entered into or adopted standardized acts that attempt to make laws regarding many issues standard within many jurisdictions. One such act is the Uniform Partnership Act. This set of statutes tries to make regulations uniform everywhere they can get legislative bodies to adopt them. The critical thing to know regarding these acts, or even state statutes, is that they have rules that attempt to regulate each specific circumstance that could arise needing a court determination. People who start a business without written agreements among the parties need to know that should a disagreement arise, the courts will look to the standard in the statute for settling the issue.

This also applies to agreements that neglect to cover a particular circumstance that may arise as a dispute. As an example, partners of a business partnership suddenly have a disagreement over how to handle the sudden incapacity of one of the Partners. The state statute affirms that he is to be replaced by the closest heir to his estate, but the Partnership Agreement calls for the remaining Partners to have the first option to purchase (buyout). The Partnership Agreement will prevail over the statute. But if the contract had failed to speak to this particular circumstance, then the statute would rule. So if you do not want the statutes to govern, make sure your agreements are comprehensive.

The Limited Partnership is an entity that consists of one or more "General Partners" and one or more "Limited Partners." It is registered with your SOS's office. In most states, the General Partner makes the application and outlines the overall purpose, name and address of the business, and "Resident Agent." The Resident Agent may be the General Partner or, in the case of a business outside the state of the General Partner's domicile, any person of legal age. A termination date is usually also required for a Partnership and most entities other than a Corporation. The law against perpetuities prevents all but Corporations from being formed to be perpetual. Some states set a maximum length of agreements, such as South Carolina at 10 years. Others just require a date, and a time span of 20 to 25 years is usually acceptable. This is not to say the business cannot exist for longer. Often an agreement will give an end date but also include a clause stating that if the parties or certain parties agree, an extension of some period or that equivalent to the first period may be elected.

The General Partnership or General Partners in a Limited Partnership have full control and manage and make all decisions. They also have full liability for the actions and debts of the company. In other words, they are personally liable and if the assets of the Partnership fall short of covering its liabilities, Creditors and suitors may look to the individual assets of the General Partners for satisfaction of any claim. Therefore, any person in a position of General Partner should consider this fact and plan their personal estate accordingly. A General Partner may have an ownership interest in the Partnership anywhere between 1% and 99%. Even with a share of only 1% or 2% ownership, a General Partner makes the decisions and manages the business despite the Limited Partners' 98% or 99% ownership. When two General Partners exist, the one with the most ownership percentage would have the final say. In the case of three or more, some board-type arrangement where the highest total interest combination in agreement on an issue would prevail. But these are issues for the written Partnership Agreement to address. Limited Partners in a Limited Partnership have limited liability. They are not allowed to participate in the management of the company. Doing so could jeopardize their limited-liability status and cause them to have full liability as a General Partner.

This is not to say that they cannot work for or in the company. A Limited Partner can also be an employee or a contractor of the business but should ensure that he is able to show his position's clear distinction from that of his ownership position.

Limited Partners also can own anywhere from 1% to 99% of the business. There can also be one, two, or many Limited Partners. Since they do not participate in management, owning more or less than another partner only amounts to a difference in the share of profit or losses that gets distributed to each partner at the end of the year. The negotiation of that limited ownership position usually comes down to the money, property, or other value brought to the business by the partner.

The Limited Partner's limited liability or risk extends to the value of assets invested or pledged to the business. For example, if you invested $50,000 into a friend or associate's business idea that he, as a General Partner, offered you for 50% of the business, your total risk would be $50,000. If his idea failed or he was sued and ended up in debt for many times that amount, his Creditors or suitors could not look to you for more. If, however, you pledged $50,000 for your 50% share and to date only paid in half that amount, the Creditors could hold you to submitting the remainder.

It should be noted that many Partnership Agreements allow the General Partner to roll the profits at year-end rather than actually distribute them. In such cases, a General Partner could use the year-end profit to expand the business. The Partners would get a report showing the profit made by the company and be required to claim that profit on their tax return even though they did not actually receive it in hand. Your Capital Account within the business would increase, much like a savings account, but your immediate use would be restricted. This clause can also work to your advantage by allowing the General Partner to protect you from the attachment or claim against your interest or profit share by a personal Creditor of yours who has obtained a "charging order."

A charging order is an order by a court allowing someone who received a judgment against you to receive the distributions from your business interest instead of you. Of course, in this case, if they receive the distribution payment, they, rather than you, are also responsible for paying the tax. So the General Partner's deferring distribution yet sending them the payment on paper only causes them a tax obligation for an amount they haven't collected. This may make them much more open to settlement and compromise.

Holding assets in a Partnership can be a good asset protection technique because the assets become the property of the Partnership itself and are no longer the individual's personal property. The individual received an ownership interest in their share of the value but no longer owns the particular assets. This means any Creditor or suitor cannot make claim to the assets because it would hurt not only you but your Partners, who the suitor has no claim against. Therefore, the best he can achieve is a charging order against your right to distribution as stipulated by the contract. If that is limited, so are the options of your adversary. This may tend to make him more agreeable to a fair settlement.

Limited Partnerships are used for a host of reasons and many business types. Lawyer's offices are often styled as Limited Partnerships as are real estate investment firms and many others. The fact that the Limited Partnership is considered a pass-through company for tax purposes makes them very appealing to individuals who do not want to be responsible for anyone else's taxes. The Limited Partnership does not pay taxes but passes the taxes on profits and losses to their individual interest holders. Additionally, Partnerships are not required to treat partners as employees; therefore, tax with-holding and Worker's Compensation Insurance are not an issue among Partners. The Partnership files a tax return on a Partner-ship 1065 Form and sends a report called a K1 to the individuals separately stating their share of income or losses, which they claim on their own personal returns. This leaves the Partnership itself free of the individual tax issues of the partners themselves.

The Limited Partnership when availed of by the members of a family may be called a Family Limited Partnership. The Family Limited Partnership can be an excellent Estate Planning tool. The family patriarch (Dad or Mom) passes the lion's share of the ownership to their children yet maintains control of the business as General Partner, with as little as a 1% ownership interest in the actual assets.

Since only the General Partner who makes application to the SOS's office is listed on public records, the names of the Limited Partners remain private. The offset for the full liability held by the General Partner is the ability to be the decision maker and to prove his business plan, product, service, or invention is sound. The drawback of full liability is no draw-back at all for the person who has properly arranged his assets and planned his estate. If you have no substantial accumulation of personally titled assets, you have little to lose. The adage, "You can't get blood from a stone," comes to mind.

The offset for the Limited Partner's lack of management control and for the risk of losing the limited amount invested is the fact that his investment, if successful, allows him a percent-age of the profits on a continuing basis until the closing date of the business venture. At that time, his principle is returned upon final dissolution.

Naturally, a large part of the appeal for or rejection of a Limited Partnership is found in the terms of the Partnership Agreement itself. Terms regarding the General Partner's ability to roll profits and withhold distribution or, conversely, a requirement to distribute them annually, will make all the difference in finding participants. The shared vision and goal of the Partners will make one attribute more or less desirable than the other. Other important considerations are buyout, death, and/or disability of Partners.

For instance, I may be perfectly happy to be Partners with my good friend but less than thrilled to have to become Partners with his wife or brother if something were to happen to him. Be sure you agree with all the terms and contingencies of the Partnership Agreement before signing on. Another contract term and unique expense item to Partnerships is the Guaranteed Payment to Partners. This may be needed when a group investing in a common idea forms a Limited Partnership. Say a group of four individuals pool $10,000 each for their business venture. Each agrees to a 25% ownership share in the business and will require at least one full-time individual to manage and spend time in pursuit of the profit to be made. If one of the four owner-Partners takes this role, the Partnership can forgo hiring an employee, doing wage reports, and withholding taxes from a salary.

Additionally, Worker's Compensation Insurance may also be waived. This is an advantage to all Partners. Yet if at year-end a profit of say, $60,000, is produced and split according to ownership share (25% each), the full-time partner may feel cheated when receiving his $15,000 (1/4 share). This is because his Partners invested only money and received the same percentage, when he contributed both his money and time. This situation is rectified by use of the Guaranteed Payment which ensures that the working partner gets paid for his time, and the company gets to take that payment as a company expense before profits are computed for the annual distribution.

While talking about expenses and profits, it should be noted here the great favoritism this system of statutory fictions provides companies of all types over that of the individual man or woman laboring to provide for themselves and their families.

A man or woman needs to attempt to obtain the highest wage or salary possible to cover the taxes on that wage and be left with enough to purchase all the things they need. On their personal tax return, very little other than mortgage interest is deductible before taxes and all else purchased after. A business, on the other hand, is just the opposite: All the income produced is first used to cover and pay for all the company needs such as rent, phones, equipment, vehicles, supplies, etc. before calculating what is left over as profit, on which a tax may be paid. This major difference will be expounded on in the coming chapters.

"Capital Accounts" are misunderstood by many individuals considering a Partnership or LLC. This confusion is somewhat mixed up with the idea of a pass-through because the company itself does not get taxed on its profits directly. Both the tax on any gains or the credit for any loss is passed on to the individual Partners themselves, usually in proportion to their ownership interest or percentage of ownership. The tax is paid on the profit received by the partner on his or her personal return each year, regardless of whether he actually receives a distribution of the profit from the company. Even if the profit is rolled back into the business, the partner claims and settles the tax on the amount he would have received.

This amount is credited within the business to the Partners' Capital Account on the "Chart of Accounts," which will be more fully discussed in another chapter. The Capital Account keeps track of each partner's contributions, earnings, and "draw" or withdrawals. A partner's contributions to the Partnership are not taxed since contributions are conceivably "Capital," or savings for which the Partner was already taxed when they were earned elsewhere. The draw or withdrawal from the Partnership is also not taxed directly as the funds conceivably come from previously deposited Capital or previously taxed earnings.

Therefore, regardless of the actual transactions in and out of the Capital Accounts, each partner receives an annual report called a K1 from the Partnership indicating his share of the profits or losses for that particular year. He then pays or receives credit on his own individual tax return according to that year's accounting figures.

Let's take a simple 50/50 Partnership, for example, and consider a scenario that will hopefully make it understandable. Bob and John start a Partnership. They each contribute $5,000 to get the business started. This is recorded in the Chart of Accounts, which, as mentioned earlier, is basically a list of account titles that a bookkeeper would set up to keep track of money flowing in and out of a business. Again, a late chapter will cover Profit & Loss and Balance Sheets a little more closely.

For now, let us give a very simple Chart of Accounts, including the Capital Accounts we are discussing (see Figure 1).

Checking	Bank	10,000.00
◦ Income (Sales)	Income	
◦ Interest Income	Other Income	
◦ Owners Equity (Total)	Equity	10,000.00
◦ Partner One (Bob) (Balance)	Equity	5,000.00
◦ Contributions	Equity	5,000.00
◦ Draw	Equity	0.00
◦ Earnings	Equity	0.00
◦ Partner Two (John) (Balance)	Equity	5,000.00
◦ Contributions	Equity	5,000.00
◦ Draw	Equity	0.00
◦ Earnings	Equity	0.00
◦ Phone	Expense	
◦ Rent	Expense	
◦ Supplies	Expense	

Figure 1: Sample Chart of Accounts

Figure 2 is a simple Profit & Loss Sheet showing one year with totals in each category and ending on December 31st, the last day of the year for this business. It reflects that Bob and John's business had sales of $50,000 with interest on bank accounts totaling $200, for a total annual income of $50,200. Additionally, it displays expenses for rent, phone, and supplies totaling $20,200, leaving a gain of $30,000 at year-end.

Bob & John's Company
Profit & Loss
January through December 2018

	Jan - Dec 18
▼ Ordinary Income/Expense	
▼ Income	
Income (Sales) ▶	50,000.00 ◀
Total Income	50,000.00
Gross Profit	50,000.00
▼ Expense	
Phone	1,800.00
Rent	14,400.00
Supplies	4,000.00
Total Expense	20,200.00
Net Ordinary Income	29,800.00
▼ Other Income/Expense	
▼ Other Income	
Interest Income	200.00
Total Other Income	200.00
Net Other Income	200.00
Net Income	30,000.00

Figure 2: Simple Profit & Loss Statement

Figure 3 is a reflection of the Balance Sheet after Bob and John started the business, each having contributed $5,000. Note that a Profit & Loss Statement keeps track of income and expenses, and a Balance Sheet keeps track of Assets, Liabilities, and Owners Equity. An important Accounting Equation for all businesses is that ASSETS = LIABILITIES + OWNERS EQUITY.

Bob & John's Company
Balance Sheet
As of December 21, 2018

	Dec 21, 18
▼ **ASSETS**	
▼ Current Assets	
▼ Checking/Savings	
Checking ▶	10,000.00 ◀
Total Checking/Savings	10,000.00
Total Current Assets	10,000.00
TOTAL ASSETS	**10,000.00**
▼ **LIABILITIES & EQUITY**	
▼ Equity	
▼ Owners Equity (Total)	
▼ Partner One (Bob) (Balance)	
Contributions	5,000.00
Total Partner One (Bob) (Balance)	5,000.00
▼ Partner Two (John) (Balance)	
Contributions	5,000.00
Total Partner Two (John) (Balance)	5,000.00
Total Owners Equity (Total)	10,000.00
Total Equity	10,000.00
TOTAL LIABILITIES & EQUITY	**10,000.00**

Figure 3: Simple Balance Sheet at Start of the Business

In the Balance Sheet in Figure 3, you will note that the $5,000 contributions from each partner are placed in the general bank account for the Company and that each partner's contribution item under Equity is credited to reflect the contribution. The Balance Sheet in Figure 4, dated December 31st, shows how the Balance Sheet in Figure 3 would be affected by the Profit & Loss Statement illustrated in Figure 2.

Figure 4, dated December 31st, shows how the Balance Sheet would be affected by the Profit & Loss Statement of

Figure 2. Notice that the net income of $30,000 after Income and Expenses, as displayed in Figure 2, is reflected in the increased asset of the bank account and, additionally, near the bottom of the Balance Sheet (Figure 4) in the category Net Income.

Bob & John's Company
Balance Sheet
As of December 31, 2018

	Dec 31, 18
▼ASSETS	
▼ Current Assets	
▼ Checking/Savings	
Checking	40,000.00 ◀
Total Checking/Savings	40,000.00
Total Current Assets	40,000.00
TOTAL ASSETS	40,000.00
▼ LIABILITIES & EQUITY	
▼ Equity	
▼ Owners Equity (Total)	
▼ Partner One (Bob) (Balance)	
Contributions	5,000.00
Total Partner One (Bob) (Balance)	5,000.00
▼ Partner Two (John) (Balance)	
Contributions	5,000.00
Total Partner Two (John) (Balance)	5,000.00
Total Owners Equity (Total)	10,000.00
Net Income	30,000.00
Total Equity	40,000.00
TOTAL LIABILITIES & EQUITY	40,000.00

Figure 4: Balance Sheet at Year End

Now, look at the Balance Sheet in Figure 5, which shows the same Balance Sheet and year-end figures. The only difference is that the date is now January 2nd of the second year in business.

Bob & John's Company
Balance Sheet
As of January 2, 2019

	Jan 2, 19
▼ ASSETS	
▼ Current Assets	
▼ Checking/Savings	
Checking	40,000.00
Total Checking/Savings	40,000.00
Total Current Assets	40,000.00
TOTAL ASSETS	40,000.00
▼ LIABILITIES & EQUITY	
▼ Equity	
Retained Earnings ▶	30,000.00 ◀
▼ Owners Equity (Total)	
▼ Partner One (Bob) (Balance)	
Contributions	5,000.00
Total Partner One (Bob) (Balance)	5,000.00
▼ Partner Two (John) (Balance)	
Contributions	5,000.00
Total Partner Two (John) (Balance)	5,000.00
Total Owners Equity (Total)	10,000.00
Total Equity	40,000.00
TOTAL LIABILITIES & EQUITY	40,000.00

Figure 5: Balance Sheet at Start of New Year

Without any additional transactions for the new year, note that the Net Income category in Figure 4 has become zero in Figure 5, to begin calculating new Income. In addition, the previous amount of $30,000 has now been placed in the Retained Earnings category, reflecting the amount that needs to be reported and split among the Partners.

Unlike a Corporation, which may indeed maintain and keep track of Retained Earnings, the Partnership will make its K1 reports and distribute these profits to the partners. This distribution may be done by either cutting checks from the business for each partner, giving him his profit share, or by keeping the funds for business use but crediting the Partners Earnings Account. A third way would be some combination of the two. Either way, the individual partner will be treated for tax purposes as though he were given all his profits.

So, for our example, let us assume the profits are held by the company and the K1 reports are readied reflecting that decision. Figure 6, again, shows the same year-end Balance Sheet with no new year transactions. The difference is the Balance Sheet is now dated January 10th and credit has been made to the Partners.

Bob & John's Company
Balance Sheet
As of January 10, 2019

	Jan 10, 19
▼ASSETS	
▼ Current Assets	
▼ Checking/Savings	
Checking	40,000.00 ◄
Total Checking/Savings	40,000.00
Total Current Assets	40,000.00
TOTAL ASSETS	40,000.00
▼LIABILITIES & EQUITY	
▼ Equity	
▼ Owners Equity (Total)	
▼ Partner One (Bob) (Balance)	
Contributions	5,000.00
Earnings	15,000.00
Total Partner One (Bob) (Balance)	20,000.00
▼ Partner Two (John) (Balance)	
Contributions	5,000.00
Earinings	15,000.00
Total Partner Two (John) (Balance)	20,000.00
Total Owners Equity (Total)	40,000.00
Total Equity	40,000.00
TOTAL LIABILITIES & EQUITY	40,000.00

Figure 6: Balance Sheet after Distributions Made to Partners

Notice also in Figure 6 that the retained earnings category is now zero and that the $30,000 amount from Figure 5 has been split between Partner One and Partner Two, with $15,000 displayed in each of their Earnings Account categories. Figure 6 shows a Total Partner Equity of $40,000, as indicated in the Total Equity line. Partner One and Partner Two Equity Lines each reflect their individual $20,000 amount. Each partner's $20,000 equity, a reflection of their initial $5,000 contribution, is added to their Earnings for the combined total. If at any time in the future the company pays out or the Partners request some amount to receive in hand, this amount will be reflected as a negative number next to the Partner's Draw category and will reduce that particular Partner's Total Equity by the amount drawn.

This allows the business to keep track of each partner separately and eliminates the need to draw in unison. The amounts drawn are not taxable events since the tax has already been paid. Figure 7 shows a date further into the year with various amounts drawn by each partner at separate times and reflecting the ongoing balances.

Bob & John's Company
Balance Sheet
As of June 30, 2019

	Jun 30, 19
▼ ASSETS	
▼ Current Assets	
▼ Checking/Savings	
Checking ▶	23,000.00 ◀
Total Checking/Savings	23,000.00
Total Current Assets	23,000.00
TOTAL ASSETS	**23,000.00**
▼ LIABILITIES & EQUITY	
▼ Equity	
▼ Owners Equity (Total)	
▼ Partner One (Bob) (Balance)	
Contributions	5,000.00
Earnings	15,000.00
Draw	-5,000.00
Total Partner One (Bob) (Balance)	15,000.00
▼ Partner Two (John) (Balance)	
Contributions	5,000.00
Earinings	15,000.00
Draw	-12,000.00
Total Partner Two (John) (Balance)	8,000.00
Total Owners Equity (Total)	23,000.00
Total Equity	23,000.00
TOTAL LIABILITIES & EQUITY	**23,000.00**

Figure 7: Balance Sheet After Some Amounts Drawn by Partners

Besides the Partnership designation for General Partnership (GP) and Limited Partnership (LP), you may also encounter the entities of Family Limited Partnership and Limited Liability Partnership (discussed briefly in Chapter 5), or even Professional Limited Partnership. Some of these variations have slightly different statutes in different jurisdictions. For example, some jurisdictions require certain licensed professions—such as doctors, architectural firms, or engineers—and others to utilize entities such as Professional Limited Partnerships or professional Corporations and restrict who can and who cannot hold ownership interests in them. Professionals who are unhappy with this play by the un-American tax agencies to keep higher-income potential earners in the highest tax brackets may need to be creative or seek individualized advice.

Finally, a note to readers who have just skimmed over this chapter and are certain they have no interest in a Partnership of any type: Maybe you have had a previous bad experience or know someone who has; if so, this may interest you. Did you know that our laws dealing with fictitious entities such as Limited Partnerships and Corporations often use the legal term "person" and very rarely mention a man or women? It's true—because men and women are real people and the law deals much more often with persons who are fictitious. In English conversation, we use the term person all the time to refer to people. In law, "Person" is a legal term and all legal terms have definitions. If you are curious enough to look, you may find a definition for "person" similar to the following: When used herein (herein referring to the law section being defined), "person" may include an individual, Partnership, LLC, Trust, or Corporation.

You will note that only artificial or fictitious entities are included in this definition of a person. I explain this to point out the fact that you do not need to go into business with your brother-in-law or some friend. You can go into business with a legal person. They are lousy companions because they can't talk, but they are great partners for the same reason.

The General Partner of your business can be you or any other living, breathing man or women, but it could also be a Corporation; Limited Partners can be an individual, Partnership, LLC, Trust, or Corporation. I say more about entity interactions in later chapters, but let me drop one sample idea here to get the gears turning.

Bill is a happily married man with a couple of children and a single-family home. He has some equity in his home and is not happy with his job. Bill has been thinking of starting his own business. After reading an informative book and deciding he doesn't want to start his business as a Sole Proprietor, he decides on a Limited Partnership. The company he is going to start is "Creative Landscapes, LP." Bill has priced the equipment and tools he needs for his business and has calculated that he will need $25,000 to get the business started. Bill realizes that, as the General Partner, he has full liability for the business, so he decides to place his only personal asset, his home, into a Family Trust. Not wanting to have a real-life partner, Bill agrees to become Partners with the Family Trust. As a legal person, the Family Trust agrees to take $25,000 from the equity of its Real Property and purchase a 50% ownership interest in "Creative Landscapes, LP." This makes Bill and the Family Trust 50/50 Partners in the new business. The business uses the $25,000 from the Family Trust's interest purchase and buys the equipment and tools needed to get started.

With this business structure, Bill has separated his personal and business tax returns from each other. He has placed assets that, as a Sole Proprietor, would be all in one basket into three separate baskets. Those being his personal basket, business basket, and trust basket, the assets of two of those baskets being no one person's assets. The assets of the business belong to both him and the Trusts. The assets of the Trust are held by a trustee, consisting of the interests of the wife and each child. This makes it very unlikely that a claimant against any one party would have a claim against all parties. They are thereby increasing asset protection.

Additionally, Bill may have improved his tax burden. As a Sole Proprietor with a gross business income of $100,000 with business expenses of $50,000, a profit of $50,000 would be the imputed income for which he would calculate his income, FICA, and Medicare taxes. He would then have to pay his home property taxes, insurance, water bill, and maintenance costs. With the arrangement chosen, the same $50,000 business costs reduce the same $100,000 gross income. However, the $50,000 profit is split between Bill and his partner, the Trust. Therefore, Bill pays income, FICA, and Medicare matching taxes on only $25,000. The other $25,000, which is the income of the Family Trust, is used to pay real estate taxes, insurance, water bill, maintenance costs, mortgage interest, and any other bills before calculating its taxable income. This remaining income, which is being passed to the wife as the first-tier beneficiary of the Trust, will be a small return on investment and have no FICA taxes associated with it. As an aside, one may note that the amount of profits after trust expenses could be adjusted with proper use of the Guaranteed Payment to Partner feature discussed earlier.

CHAPTER 6

Joint Venture

A "Joint Venture" is not necessarily an entity type of its own. The word "Joint" denotes two or more, and the word "Venture" denotes being exposed to or taking a risk. Therefore, Joint Venture is two or more individuals taking a risk. This is a fair assessment of any Partnership, but a business Joint Venture is typically a General or Limited Partnership entered for a specific purpose for a limited time.

The Joint Venture may be entered into by two or more individuals or two or more of any entity or business type and any combination of them. These may include two long-existing businesses, each successful and separate from each other in every way, that decide for some mutual benefit to join forces for a particular purpose and or time. It may be that they each brings different strengths or expertise to the table. It may be to combine resources or share risk or any combination of those. The very act of joining together for a project establishes a Partnership relationship, although this does not necessarily dictate the formation of a statutory General or Limited Partnership.

For longer-term ventures, the formation of an LLC, Trust, or Corporation may be formed with an agreed-upon split of ownership interests, such as stock holdings in a Corporation, along with some agreement regarding board or management control. The search for cures for certain diseases, mineral deposits, and gas and oil explorations are just a few of the many reasons individuals and companies have joined together.

CHAPTER 7

Association

An "Association" is an organization of persons. A group in society or, for our purposes, a group or organization, come together for a business purpose. Technically, this could refer to every entity other than the Sole Proprietorship and the single-person LLC. The IRS uses it as a catch-all term for business organizations not specifically defined as a General Partnership or Limited Partnership or otherwise excluded as a Corporation, Trust, or Estate under the definition of a Partnership, as outlined in section 761 of Title 26 of the United States Code. The term "Partnership" includes a syndicate, group, pool, joint venture, or other unincorporated organization through or by means of which any business, financial operation, or venture is carried on.

In other words, if you do business with another person or group of persons, whether with or without a written agreement, and you are not registered as another specific type of statutory entity such as a Corporation, you may be considered an Association. As an Association, you are considered a Partnership and are required to file for and report income as such. Remember, a Partnership is a pass-through tax organization and by itself does not owe a tax but passes the tax on to the individuals involved. Partnerships report income to the IRS on

Form 1065 Partnership Return and report the pass-through income to the Partners on K1 Forms or a substitute for K1s.

There are exceptions to this classification if the individuals so choose. Any Partnership that is availed of for real estate and/or investment purposes only, and not for an active service or product, may be excepted from the definition of a Partnership under section 761a. This applies if the number of Partners is less than 10 and all are individuals or corporations whose individual share of income is a simple process to determine.

As stated in a previous chapter, the Constitution for the united States of America guarantees the right to contract. That being the case, many prefer the option of outlining the terms of their business ventures with others by creatively constructing agreements that cover all the conceivable considerations for their working and business relationship, including any profit sharing, transfer, and control rights. These agreements may be referred to simply as contracts. Although they may resemble and be similar in conduct to some of the registered statutory forms, they are considered non-statutory. They are sometimes referred to by various other names such as "Business Trusts," "Contract Trusts," "Unincorporated Business Organization" or "UBO," "Pure Trust Organization" or "PTO," "Constitutional Trusts," and several other names.

These organizations offer many advantages and conveniences, a few of which include ease in changing jurisdiction and venue, low fees as they have no annual state fees or annual reports due, as well as good privacy for their members. A disadvantage is the lack of understanding by other statutory entities that may interact with them. Obtaining bank loans and credit can be cumbersome. Additionally, because of their misuse by some groups, certain names like Pure Trust, etc. may cause a suspicious eye to be cast by certain government agencies. Although these organizations are both lawful and legal and have been utilized by some very familiar names and long-standing companies and financial institutions, you should seek sound advice regarding their use.

Unfortunately, in the last 20 or so years, some individuals within the "Patriot Community" or "Constitutional Movement" have been less than scrupulous. These groups and movements, for the most part, are wonderful grassroots organizations fighting to maintain citizen rights, our Constitutional Amendments, and Bill of Rights. A few among them, however, make a living merchandising certain legal theories that have caused many great harm and heartache.

These are sellers of Pure Trust Organizations, Constitutional Trusts, and the like. Claims are made that these entities are tax-free and that their business earnings have no income tax liabilities. Many people are urged to divert their personal income into and through them, which magically is supposed to eliminate the tax liability. When trouble comes, these people will not be there with you in court. These purveyors of snake oil are at best lazy and misinformed and at worst outright shysters.

Again, to make sure I am not misquoted, the Pure Trust and Constitutional Trusts themselves are both lawful and legal. In fact, some are wonderfully creative, and they can be put to many great uses. It is not a lie that they have no tax liability of their own. The IRS considers them a "Disregarded Entity" and does not look for a tax return from them. That said, this does not mean the IRS or various state agencies do not consider that the individuals involved with them do not have tax liabilities on taxable events. If you receive taxable income from taxable sources and engage in taxable activities, there is a tax to be paid—whether or not you pass it through a Disregarded Entity before or after the transaction! According to the IRS, a single-person LLC, for example, is also a Disregarded Entity. But you can be sure that if your LLC is used to bring you taxable income whether or not the LLC pays it to you, you are still taxed. Similarly, the Pure Trust and Constitutional Trust or UBO has little to do with whether the value received is taxable or not taxable. Gross Income sources and certain activities determine tax liability, not necessarily entity type.

When dealing with the IRS and taxes, remember the saying "Substance over Form." Remembering this will help keep you safe. You can write whatever you want on paper, but if that is not what is really taking place, then it is just "form" and they will look to the "substance" of the actual events.

For example, let's say I place my home in trust for the benefit of my children. Let's also say I want to make sure the trust has money for maintenance and upkeep. I ask the person I am receiving taxable income from to cut checks directly to the Trust. Can I do that? Is it legal? Yes, I can do that, and yes, it is legal. What is not legal is for me to claim it as a Pure Trust Income and not taxable. As long as I declare the income on my tax return and pay the tax, I can save or give my money to whomever I want. Even if it is a Pure Trust, considered a disregarded entity by the IRS. Again, it is the nature of the transaction and not the entity itself. Caveat Emptor. Buyer Beware.

CHAPTER 8

Corporation

A "Corporation" is a legal creation authorized to act with the rights and liabilities of a person; in other words, a legal fictitious person. Individuals are permitted by the state to act or carry on business together as if they were a single body. Today many states allow an individual alone to operate as a Corporation or to Incorporate.

Technically, the group that makes up the Corporate Body consists of its incorporator, director and/or board of directors, officers, and stockholders. However, as noted, many states allow one person to hold all these positions individually and still be considered a Corporation.

The individual that submits the Article of Incorporation and makes application to the SOS's office, in whichever state he chooses to Incorporate, is the Incorporator. This individual may be the original owner or party interested in seeing the company started or may just be a person from a company that aids others in opening a Corporation.

Corporations are owned by their stockholders; this may be one person or many. These persons may be individuals, Partnerships, Trusts, or other Corporations. The state of Incorporation usually sets the number of "Authorized Shares" a Corporation may have. In some states, it may be 1,000 shares;

in others, the standard may be set at 10,000, 25,000, or some other amount. A person can pay a fee or tax and request increased amounts of stock above the standard. They can do this from the start, or they may add more as the need arises. This number of shares is referred to as Authorized Shares. The portion of this amount at any one time in the hands of individual stockholders is considered the "Issued Shares." The number and ratio of "Issued Shares" to current stockholders is what determines the percentage of ownership a stockholder is considered to hold. For example, you and a friend decide to start a Corporation; it comes with 10,000 Authorized Shares. If You want to be 50/50 owners, how should the stock be handled? Well, you could each take 5,000 shares, but then all Authorized Stock would become "Issued Stock." Alternatively, you could each take as little as 100 shares. You would still be 50/50 owners of the Corporation as you each would hold 50% of the Issued Stock. The remaining 9,800 shares would be held in reserve for future use. "Issued Stocks" are those shares taken from the total amount of Authorized Shares and distributed to owners, investors, or stock purchasers.

In another example, let's say you and your friend from the last scenario are planning on selling some of the stock in the Corporation to raise capital to run the business. In this case, you may want to each take 2,501 shares, making your combined total 5,002 shares—just over 50% of the Authorized Shares. This will ensure that even if you sell and issue the remaining 4,998 shares, you and your friend together maintain over 50% of the ownership. This will keep both of you in control of the company and able to outvote all other ownership interests. In addition, this position will keep you in control of the director and, in turn, of your officers handling the day-to-day operations of the business. Of course, if you individually apply the same principle of maintaining control and majority ownership for yourself, no friend or partner is necessary.

At times, Corporations have been known to buy back some of their outstanding stock. When this is done the stock is held in treasury and called "Treasury Stock." Most small closed Corporations issue to all one type of stock called "Common Stock." Some Corporations, however, may offer "Preferred Stock" as well as Common Stock, establishing various rights or privileges to one type over the other. Preferred stockholders receive an extra or priority dividend over Common stockholders.

Typically, a stock's value is the actual value of the company divided by the outstanding Issued shares. However, stocks often sell at amounts below and often way above this value. Determining the value of assets themselves can be hard enough, but when adding factors like "Good Will," "potential Market Share," in-process "Research and Development," "Earnings and Debts," and a host of other factors, it can become outright conjecture. IBM, Microsoft, and Apple are among the many companies whose public shares are traded on the Stock Exchange Market, which is governed and controlled by the Securities and Exchange Commission, a government agency. But for the purposes of this book, we will stick with the small Corporation. Most start-ups have Common Stock with no-par value assigned to a share. Some small Corporations do disclose an initial capitalization, pay a fee, and establish a par value per share—this value is governed by the capital amount and the number of shares.

For our purposes, you should know that the stockholders own the Corporation. The ownership share is in proportion to the percentages of stock owned against that Issued, with an eye on what amount is available to issue; these are called "Authorized Shares." Your corporate book should include a stock ledger, which is merely a method of keeping track of name and address and number of shares bought, sold, or transferred on what date for what amount.

If you intend to raise capital for the company to get off the ground or at some point to expand or grow, you need to be aware that rules exist governing such things. A visit to the Securities and Exchange Commission's website can provide relevant information. If you remain under certain minimums, you will stay outside of the jurisdiction of the SEC. Typically, people raise funds from family, friends, or business associates—sometimes in the hundreds of thousands of dollars. As long as you keep the number of participants under 35, you won't run into any problems. If you get into higher numbers or use media advertising, you have definitely crossed that line and most certainly should seek legal advice. Consumer protection laws protect the public. You should know that there are people called "Accredited Investors" who are seen as knowledgeable and able to make decisions for themselves. These people have certain thresholds of assets and/or a certain minimum annual income. People below these means are considered to be in need of protection. Later, if they complain about you and your company not performing as previously anticipated, you may have a big headache and wish you never dealt with them.

All the stockholders of your company, whether or not they

have a controlling interest, are entitled to be notified of your annual board meeting and stockholders' meetings. They are also entitled to a Profit & Loss Statement and Balance Sheet. If you neglect these rights, you may hear from their attorneys. Starting your business on other people's money can be a blessing or a curse. Such decisions are not to be taken lightly.

Raising capital by selling shares of stock has the advantage of gaining funds that in theory do not need to be paid back like a loan. The company has no obligation to buy back its stock at any time, although it may want to at some point. The stockholder invests his funds in anticipation of dividends in the future, along with an increase in the value of his stock that can later be sold to yet another interested party, to receive a buyout offer, or, lastly, to receive his share of the company assets at dissolution. The advantages of stock over a loan is that if plans progress slower than expected, the lack of required payments could help financial survival.

The advantage of funding the company with loans is that you do not have to sell off any ownership in the company nor share future profits with multiple owners. The disadvantage of loans is the payback schedule of principle and interest, which draws against the company's early income. If progress and growth are behind schedule, you may go out of business or forfeit ownership to the lenders.

Okay, so the Incorporator incorporates the business, and the stockholders own it. Now the stockholders elect or appoint a director who in turn elects, appoints, or suggests a slate of officers to fill the position of president, vice president, treasurer, and secretary. These officers may be part of the board of directors along with the director, or you may have a board of directors apart from the officers. The director(s) oversee the general direction of the company and make major decisions. The officers then implement these decisions and resolutions on a day-to-day basis, running the company and supervising employees and operations. At least yearly, and more frequently if called for, an annual meeting of the board of directors should be held. In close proximity, an annual meeting of the stockholders should also be convened, and proper notice should be given to each. Major decisions and any changes in policy or company strategy, along with copies of Profit & Loss and Balance Sheets and Tax Returns covering previous periods, should be presented. You should also ask for a vote to either continue the term of the officers or vote any appropriate changes. Even in companies that have as little as one person wearing all the hats of management, the corporate book and records should be kept up to date and in order. Without a log of meetings, resolutions, and other documents, the first attack by opposing attorneys on your corporate limited liability will be an attempt to show you are not acting as a Corporation.

Concerning naming conventions, long-held terms such as officer, president, vice president, treasurer, and secretary are rapidly being replaced with such titles as "CEO" for chief executive officer, "CFO" for chief financial officer, and many others.

The participants in a Corporation all have limited liability when acting in good faith to carry on the business of the company. Short of either extreme negligence or a criminal act, limited liability protects the directors and officers from personal liabilities and complainants and suitors cannot rightly reach personal assets for the satisfaction of damages. This also applies to stockholders because, as stockholders, they do not manage the company. Of course, the Corporation and its assets would be available to satisfy any judgment won by a suitor. This may, in turn, lead to lost jobs, reduced stock value, or even business failure. However, limited liability means the complainant or suitor cannot look beyond the Corporation's own assets to those of the officers or stockholders.

The Corporate statutes in most states are very similar, but there are some differences. Most states allow for a single individual to start and run a Corporation, but there are those that do not. Such things as "Bearer Shares" and other privacy issues make some states a more desirable location to organize a Corporation than others. A state's start-up and annual fees along with their corporate tax rates also govern desirability.

Some favorite states—those that have no state corporate income taxes and favorable privacy laws—include Delaware, Nevada, and Wyoming. If you choose to incorporate your business in one of these states and you are not a resident personally, then you will need a Resident Agent. Many individuals and companies provide these services in each state as a business service. Resident Agent services are explained in more detail in Chapter 1.

Your company is considered to be a "Domestic Corporation" in the state in which it incorporates. Then depending on its activities in other states, it may have to register as a "Foreign Corporation." Most states other than Wyoming usually require the corporate indicator of Incorporated, Limited, Corporation, or their abbreviations Inc., Ltd., or Corp. after the Company name. Again, see Chapter 1 for a discussion of names and company registrations.

Unlike other entity types, Corporations can be perpetual. This means they do not have to have a planned ending date; they can go on and on and outlive their individual participants. This attribute can be a great personal Estate Planning tool.

Corporations, being artificial or fictitious persons in the legal context, need real people to speak and act on their behalf as they cannot do so for themselves. This is why directors and officers are necessary. These participants speak and act on behalf of the Corporation with regard to fulfilling its goals and purposes, as outlined in its Articles of Incorporation using the guidelines of its bylaws and maintaining a record of its actions and decisions in minutes and resolutions. The Corporate Books consist of this ongoing record of minutes of the meetings and resolutions, together with Incorporation papers, the stock ledger, and financial and tax records.

For an individual participant to maintain their protection of limited liability, major decisions about banking, investments, product lines, etc. should be reflected in the minutes and resolutions of the Company. This shows that actions were the corporate acts of the Corporation and not the acts of an individual.

As stated, "Public Corporations" are owned and traded by the public on the Stock Exchange, while small private Corporations are held privately and called "Close Corporations." Some of these so-called small Corporations, however, may be far from what many people would describe as small; those with assets in the many millions of dollars fall into this class. Just as with the Professional Partnership, there also are Professional Corporations with the same or similar objectives, as stated in Chapter 5. Like the others, these may limit the type of participants that can be stockholders or directors.

Undoubtedly you have heard of many other names such as Holding Corporations, Shell Corporations, Personal Holding Corporations, Front Companies, Non-Profit Corporations, C and S Corporations, and several others. Most of these, however, refer to your typical Corporation as outlined in this chapter. The different descriptions by which they are referred have more to do with their function, purpose, or tax classification than being a different entity type. For instance, a Shell Corporation tends to have its stock held by another company whose stock is owned by yet another company. This attempt to make the ultimate owner or beneficiary of the company difficult to recognize reminds some of the game of hiding a pea under one of three shells. The observer is challenged to pick the right shell after they are rearranged on the surface; hence, Shell Corporation. Movies, politicians, and Big Brother government agencies like to focus on some of the illegitimate uses and motives of these types of companies while disregarding their many legitimate uses.

When a Corporation—or any statutory entity, for that matter—comes to an end or dissolves, there is usually a statute requiring notification of some type, which may include a fee. Whether voluntary or involuntary, the requirements for ending a business have priorities that need to be adhered to. The assets of a company need first to be used to pay off secured Creditors and then non-secured Creditors. Only after these debts are paid are the remaining assets liquidated or distributed to the ownership interest holders in their respective portions; in a Corporation, this would be the stockholder. Whether this is an increase or decrease from your original capital investment will determine your tax consequences.

Corporations file income tax returns annually. Those whose fiscal year is the calendar year are required to file their return for the previous calendar years' income by March 15th of the current year. There is a simple one-page extension request that can be made for an automatic six-month extension. Many companies with accountants who prepare individual returns in time for April 15th regularly use the extension to spread out their work schedules and tax preparation season. Probably more Corporations avail themselves of an extension than don't so you should not fear that this will make you more likely to be selected for an audit. In fact, it's probably the opposite.

The fiscal years of many Corporations, especially municipal and governmental ones, do not correspond to the civic calendar year. Typically, they start at one of the civic calendar quarter points such as June 1st or October 1st. Depending on the industry or the ownership of more than one business, there are reasons for doing so. I prefer the calendar year for simplicity.

Corporations file Federal Corporate Tax Return Form 1120 or 1120S and their corresponding state forms, if any, are required. A Corporation fitting the definition of "doing business within the state" in more than one state may be required to register as a Foreign Corporation in such states. When this is the case, keeping track of sales and income from various jurisdictions may be important. In such instances, income may need to be apportioned to the various states. Basically, that means you pay each state for the income received from within it but not from elsewhere; this reduces the amount paid to your home state where the Corporation was domesticated.

The difference between a C Corporation and an S Corporation has to do with an application that can be made to the IRS for S Corporation status. This is done immediately, following incorporation, when requesting your Taxpayer or Employer Identification Number (TIN / EIN). If you do not make the application, your Corporation will be a C Corporation. For an S Corporation status, certain conditions apply. Namely, your stockholders are restricted to individuals, estates, and specific qualified trusts.

S Corporations allow for a pass-through tax situation much like a Partnership. This means the Corporation will not have to pay a tax on the company's profits and then have the owners pay another tax when receiving those profits as income. It removes the so-called double taxation of the C Corporation. This can be desirable for owners who want to receive W2 wages as their earned income, as opposed to a Partnership where they might make estimated quarterly deposits and compute the resulting tax at year-end. These owners will still be responsible for paying taxes on dividends if they draw randomly during the year, have profits in excess of their salaries, or make personal expenditures using the business checking account.

Businesses with low-capital-start-up needs and a low-overhead-to-personal-income ratio should undoubtedly consider the S Corporation over the C Corporation. But they should also recognize that there is a less distinct line between business and personal compared to some other options. Also, certain asset protection techniques may be limited due to the restriction on stockholder types.

The C Corporation is a wholly distinct person in a legal

sense—a body made up of its various members with no one individual being the Corporation itself. A C Corporation takes its income and deducts all expenses from it, including depreciation of its assets and amortization of start-up costs, research and development, and other intangibles. The resulting profits or losses are that of the company itself. The company pays a tax on its profits or receives a credit for any losses to be carried forward and used against profits in future years. These profits, when held by the company, become "Retained Earnings"; a C Corporation can retain its earnings up to a certain amount. This may be done to have a buffer against lean business times, to plan an expansion, or to replace equipment and assets that will be needed in the future. Typically, the IRS allows the retention of earnings up to $250,000 without a specific reason. Larger amounts may incur a tax penalty, the purpose of which is to pressure the company to declare a dividend or distribute profits to its stockholders.

This is done not so much because the IRS favors stockholders over the company but because the company has already paid tax on its profits, and the IRS now wants those profits passed to the individual so they can tax them again as income to the stockholders. If the company were to accrue these already-taxed profits for long periods or perpetually, the second tax would not be applied. Hence, the tax penalty at a certain point.

This double taxation usually referred to by those who caution against the C Corporation as an entity for the small business owner is not always the detriment it is made out to be. Although it could change the Corporate tax rate, which is, as of this writing, 15% on the first $50,000 of profit per year. Profits above this figure are subject to increasingly higher rates applied at various thresholds until reaching the individual tax rate, around 38%.

Many are the numbers of small business owners who have been steered away from the C Corporation due to the so-called double taxation. They are often told they are too small or do not foresee profits large enough to make it worthwhile. This is just poor advice and/or lack of understanding, which is essentially the same thing. In fact, the small C Corporation probably has an advantage over the larger. Higher and faster profits of the large company increase its tax rate toward the highest end. It's the first $50,000 per year that is taxed at only 15%. That means that profits of $50,000 per year could be retained in the Corporation as savings for up to five years before reaching the threshold for distribution. All of these profits are taxed at a 15% rate—one of the lowest that exists. These funds additionally are held outside an individual's estate. (Read separate basket: Asset Protection.) Should the business experience lean times, losses are filled in with available funds rather than an additional infusion of capital from previously higher-taxed savings. Moreover, said losses would allow for carrying forward credit against future gains that replenish the retained earnings at no additional tax.

Even if the company pays a 15% tax on profits and then distributes them to the individual as a dividend, this dividend tax added to the 15% tax only brings the so-called double taxation to about the rate for an individual having taken all the income as a Sole Proprietor. These rules were designed by the IRS to prevent the individual from just turning their personal incomes into lower-taxed corporate earnings. Therefore, that portion of income that is unavoidably double-taxed only experiences the same rate that it would have had the C Corporation entity type not been chosen in the first place. Yet by selecting the C Corporation, you can realize numerous other advantages including those previously described.

Additionally, the salaries of owners who are also stockholders can be deducted as an expense. So by adjusting salary and bonuses, you can adjust company profits. For example, ABC Company has sales of $100,000 this year. If expenses are $60,000 of that, then $40,000 might be the company's profit and therefore taxed. But if the owner of ABC sets his salary at $40,000, then that adds $40,000 to ABC's expenses, leaving the company zero profit. Although the owner will be taxed on his personal income, the company has no tax. So here you have a C Corporation with no double-taxation issue. This example does not even begin to touch upon the advantages of fringe benefits and company perks, which are all deductible expenses for the company but are not taxable as income to the individual corporate officer or employee.

Perks include such things as company-provided vehicles, cell phones, laptops and desktop computers, health benefits, tuition reimbursement, and memberships—and, at times, housing, travel, meals, entertainment, and seminars and professional development. All these things, including retirement plans and so forth, cut down company profits and thereby tax on profits. They also reduce the need for duplication of these same things in the individual's personal life. Hence the need for higher salaries with higher taxes can be avoided. Why go out and make purchases with after-tax dollars from your salary for things that can be provided to you with before-tax dollars? The C Corporation is definitely a viable choice for an entity type for both small and large companies alike. A successful business, as well as estate and asset protection plans, can be yours by creatively coupling the C Corporation with stockholding Trusts or other Corporations. Tax savings, Family Dynasty, and inheritance issues can all find their advantages in the proper use of the C Corporation.

Although the preceding was written before the 2018 tax changes, and the Corporate tax rate is now a flat 22%, the principle of being careful about so-called conventional wisdom still applies. And the C Corporation is still an excellent tool for a small-business entity choice. To learn how the new tax laws affect any of the various topics discussed in this book, be sure to check the appendices and the suggested business websites for updates and related articles.

CHAPTER 9

Limited Liability Company

The "Limited Liability Company," known as an "LLC," is a statutory creation arising from the supposed shortfall of both the Corporation and the Limited Partnership. It is somewhat of a hybrid of the two and has become very popular in recent years.

Unfortunately, that popularity has led it to have some of the highest registration costs and annual fees among the entity types. As with most, registration takes place at the SOS's office in whichever state you desire to do business.

LLCs have Managing Members and Members. Like the Limited Partnership has one or more General Partners, the LLC has one or more Managing Members—the corresponding position. The difference, however, is that the Managing Member has limited liability. The position corresponding to the Limited Partner in the Limited Partnership is that of the Member in the LLC. Since many states also allow for a single-member LLC, unlike the Limited Partnership needing one or more Limited Partners, the LLC can have none or one or more Members. Like Limited Partners, LLC Members enjoy limited liability. Unlike them, however, they are also allowed to participate in management without loss of limited liability.

Therefore, like the Corporation, the Members of LLCs all

have limited liability yet, unlike the Corporation, do not have the so-called double taxation issue. The LLC has the option to either file a tax return like a Corporation or file as a pass-through like a Partnership. This option needs to be chosen with care as the IRS makes it difficult to change. The single-person LLC, however, does not have these options. For its purposes, the IRS considers the single-person LLC to be a "Disregarded Entity." Therefore, the individual files for his LLC using Schedule C, which is attached to his personal income tax return in the same way as that of a Sole Proprietor.

For this reason, as with the Sole Proprietor, I am not usually a fan of the single-person LLC as it marries your business and personal interests, tying them too closely together. Like the Limited Partnership, if you desire an LLC and are not consider-ing other individuals for Partners, you can still have a multi-person LLC by simply becoming Partners with another artifi-cial person. A second company of yours or a Family Trust created with even limited assets may serve the purpose.

Like the Limited Partnership, the LLC spreads out owner-ship interests totaling 100% among its Members. This can be done in numerous ways and percentages, depending on the number of both managing and non-managing members. Unlike the Corporation, in which it is easy to issue additional stock to effect ownership changes or to add other parties, the changes to LLC ownership can be a little more cumbersome. For example, let's say you are the Managing Member of an LLC, own a 40% interest, and have two limited members who each own 30%. As Managing Member, you call the shots and manage the business according to the LLC's operating agreement. You become interested in attracting a person who could greatly benefit the company or maybe infuse desperately needed capital. How will you do it? Will each member agree and give up a percentage of their ownership interest to the new party? Even if all parties agree, this usually means the rewriting of the LLC's contract between the parties and an adjustment to capital accounts. This increases the expense and time, as attorneys and accountants become involved.

The operating agreement of an LLC, which is an essential feature of the business most especially when dealing with other Members that are indeed separate from you. Remember, generalized statutes will take precedence over all issues not explicitly addressed in the original agreement should a disagreement arise. So the distribution of profits, buy-out issues, death, and disability of members and many other issues are important to include. Shared expectations are the best way to avoid disagreement. Having a professionally prepared agreement should undoubtedly be considered.

At first glance, the hybrid feature of the LLC—its ability to avoid the double taxation issues that come with the Corporation and the liability issue specific to the General Partner of the Limited Partnership—may lead you to believe it's the hands-down choice. But the higher costs of both fees and contract change necessitated by the LLC, along with the fact that it cannot be perpetual like the Corporation, should be considered. Additionally, the full liability of the General Partner in a Limited Partnership need not be the deterrent it appears. With proper personal asset planning or the use of an artificial General Partner such as a Corporation, the drawback can be mitigated.

Both of these entities have much longer and more solid case

histories in the courts, with precedents on many issues. Where the LLC has the advantage of limited liability for all, it also has a drawback: limited members who participate in management are open to suit by claims of negligence. It's my opinion that in today's environment, the courts may see the popularity of the LLC as a reason to lessen rather than strengthen regard for the inviolable features of limited liability.

CHAPTER 10

Contracts

As previously stated, our Constitution, Article I, section 10, guarantees us that the right to contract shall not be impaired. What constitutes a Contract and makes it legally binding? A "Contract" is a binding agreement between two or more parties setting forth the rights and benefits as well as the duties, responsibilities, and obligations of each party—called terms—along with the time frame for the performance. Contracts need to be entered into knowingly, intentionally, and willingly. A Contract that a person is forced into is said to be agreed to under duress or coercion and is not lawfully enforceable, since it is no Contract at all. Additionally, Contracts in which some terms are hidden by or from a party are not legally binding. The Supreme Court has ruled that fraud corrupts all that it touches, making void such agreements.

Generally, there are five parts of a Contract. They are the Offer, Acceptance, Consideration, Competency, and Legality. All five are needed to make an agreement legally binding on the parties involved. Although they are binding whether verbal or written, a contract is difficult to enforce if it is not written. A verbal agreement witnessed or admitted to by the parties constitutes a Contract. Most jurisdictions have a law referred to as the "Statute of Frauds," which states that all contracts above a certain value must be in writing to be enforceable. This amount varies and may be as low as $500. Now, this does not mean that an agreement above said value is not a legal contract; it simply means that the courts in a given jurisdiction will not be obligated to hear an argument regarding the law or help you to enforce it.

Every day, verbal unwritten agreements meeting all five criteria are closed and completed very quickly, sometimes with hardly even a word exchanged. An example is going to a supermarket and picking up a gallon of milk displayed for sale at $2 (the Consideration), and the clerk Accepting it (Acceptance) and bagging the milk for you to carry away. You both appear Competent (Competency) and, of course, the sale and purchase of milk being legal (Legality), the whole agreement is entered into, performed, and completed in just a couple of minutes.

Written agreements can range from simple to extremely complicated and everything in between. For instance, the purchase of a home is an agreement that is more complicated and takes place over time in stages. A homeowner will make known his willingness to Accept Offers on his property by putting out a sign or employing a Real Estate Agent. An interested buyer makes an Offer to purchase the home at a particular price. This shows he is clear about what he is willing to pay and by when he may include specific terms to the agreement. Such terms can include things like his Offer needing to be Accepted by a specific date and issues like making sure that the appliances come with the house, that he has the right to check the foundation for cracks or the walls for termites, or that his bank will lend the funds. If these terms and price are agreeable to the seller, he will Accept the Offer, and a Purchase and Sale Agreement will be entered into that includes all the agreed-upon terms and time frames.

Some amount of money called a Deposit is generally put up along with the Purchase and Sales Agreement. Usually a part of the terms is placing the deposit, maybe $500 to $1,000, in escrow with the agent or Title Company. This Deposit is to make the parties legally bound to follow through with the agreement by adding the criteria of Consideration, which would otherwise be lacking and render the contract unenforceable. Since selling a home is legal and the parties, appearing to all be competent responsible adults of legal age, the Competency and Legality criteria are met at the time of Offer and Acceptance. In most cases, this leaves some form of Consideration the final factor in making a binding agreement. Obviously, agreements between drug dealers for drugs, thieves for stolen goods, or any number of other criminal acts, whether written or verbal, are not legally binding contracts.

When entering into an agreement, you may find the issue of Competency to be one of the more obscure parts of the contract; the other four are straightforward. Competency, for the most part, is presumed between consenting adults who are not otherwise obviously incompetent. You should know that although it is not illegal to enter into an agreement with a minor, should you do so you are bound to the terms and the minor is not. A minor can change their mind about an agreement and cannot be held in breach, so that should be taken into consideration. Also, if a person is apparently under the influence of alcohol or drugs, it is incumbent upon you to recognize that they are not competent to enter a contract.

A mentally disabled or handicapped individual may also not be held accountable or competent to enter agreements. If you enter into contracts with such individuals, the contracts may not be null and void automatically, and you will most likely be held to perform even though the person could be released.

The rule-of-thumb criterion here is to be sure you can argue that any or most reasonable men and women would have come to the same conclusion. There are certain circumstances under which most people of average intelligence would be considered competent to enter into an agreement. However, you may want to go the extra mile to protect yourself by having additional witnesses and/or explicit disclosure statements and disclaimers. An example would be selling financial or investment opportunities or products to anyone not well versed in such areas, especially the very old or very young. Another might be selling extremely technical or scientific products, services, or opportunities. Successfully entering into an agreement or selling a product or service to someone you know, or suspect does not fully understand all the terms or ramifications is a recipe for disaster. The long-term health of you and your business are not worth any one-time sale or score.

A few more caveats regarding contracts should be kept in mind. If an agreement or form needs your signature, *it is voluntary!* It is probably an offer to contract or to subject yourself to some agreement or agency. READ what you sign! If you are uncertain get advice *before* you sign; afterward is too late. Most agreements are bilateral, meaning both sides agree on all terms, and are required to enable any terms of the contract to be changed at a later date. Unilateral contracts may be entered into voluntarily by parties agreeing to mutual terms. But in unilateral agreements, one party may change the terms and the other party may remain bound to the contract. Be aware and wary of such agreements and look carefully for them when dealing with certain multinational Corporations— most especially, banks, financial institutions, and government agencies.

Before closing out this chapter, I would like to mention a couple of other agreements that can be very convenient and beneficial at times yet have the potential to be quite detrimental if not used cautiously.

The first is the "Power of Attorney." Both full and limited Powers of Attorney can be given by an individual to another individual, enabling the "Attorney-in-Fact." This means that an individual receives the Power to act for another on behalf of the "Principle" (the individual giving the permission) to take actions, decide matters, enter agreements, or do anything the Principle could otherwise do for him or herself. This can be done by giving another person permission to act on your behalf in a specific matter, such as selling a piece of Real Estate. This would be a "Limited Power of Attorney" confined to a specific event(s) or for a certain period of time; if, for instance, you owned a property in Florida but lived in New England and would not be able to attend the closing of the sale of said property. You might allow your sister or friend who lives nearby in Florida to attend the closing and sign all documents on your behalf. The sister or friend would present the Limited Power of Attorney to display her authority to act on your behalf in the matter.

The "Durable" or full "Power of Attorney" may be extended to a trusted individual to carry out any matter on your behalf. A possible reason might be a serviceman going overseas giving "Power of Attorney" to his wife or a parent to handle his affairs while he is away and unavailable to do so himself. Husband and Wife may exchange Powers of Attorney with each other to protect against the incapacity of one or the other. Numerous examples could be given.

As you can imagine, a great deal of responsibility and trust go along with these instruments. Those parties such as banks, Real Estate Agents, etc. who rely on your permission for these individuals to act as your Attorney-in-Fact are not responsible for his or her actions. In fact, quite the opposite. It is not anyone else's place to police the actions of your Attorney, it is yours. That is why these Powers should not be given lightly. If you are contemplating divorce or have any issue regarding trust, do not agree to this. If it is unavoidable that you trust someone, give out a Limited or Specific Power that ends or expires after a particular act.

By law, a person receiving a Power-of-Attorney is supposed to act in the interest of the person giving it, but such things can sometimes be subjective or opinionated. If you decide to terminate Powers previously provided, you should do so in writing. It is also wise to notify anyone, such as a bank, to whom the Attorney-in-Fact presented it. Even though the party you gave permission to may be liable for misusing it, if they have lost or spent all your money and are without the means to make restitution it will be you who suffers.

A "Nominee Agreement" can be convenient for managing affairs while you are absent, or for privacy and anonymity. In these agreements, again, the Principle—a person having actual ownership or rights to a title or position, due to either absence or a desire to remain anonymous or avoid controversy or conflict—may use another person as his agent to act, appear to act, own, or hold some asset, business, position, or title as a Nominee.

These agreements should be carefully considered, taking into account many factors such as confidentiality clauses that may need to extend beyond the terms of the general agreement. The roles of each party, including the consequences for breach of contract, should be clearly delineated. In addition, the agreement should include a detailed listing of the actual assets, fees, and income split involved, including any interest whatsoever actually held by the nominee.

For example, let's assume an unknown individual who has a good amount of Capital and is a great cook decides to open a restaurant in New York City. Let's call him Jeff the Chef. Jeff knows a famous New York Yankee baseball player named Tom Walker. Jeff proposes to Tom to open a restaurant and bar called Walker's Place. He will own and finance it all but would like to make it appear that Walker owns the place, being sure the name will draw crowds. Tom Walker agrees that for 20% of the profits and no responsibility to work the business he is willing to represent himself as the owner of the company, and even agrees to make an appearance several times a month. He agrees further to supply a display case with some trophies and other memorabilia. An agreement is drawn up, and Tom Walker becomes a nominee owner for Jeff the Chef.

Now, they each have concerns that need to be addressed. Jeff the Chef needs to be sure that Tom Walker will not eventually actually claim the business is his and try to sell it or borrow against its value. Tom Walker doesn't want Jeff the Chef telling people on the q.t. that he is really the owner and make Tom look bad. Additionally, Tom wants it listed in the agreement that although he owns nothing else, his sports trophies and memorabilia are his property.

Certainly, there would be many issues to consider besides those mentioned, and there are numerous other examples and reasons for the use of Nominee Agreements. Hopefully, this example gives some indication of not only the possible convenience but also the potential danger of ill-considered or poorly written agreements.

Nominee Agreements are legal if used for a lawful purpose. You should bear in mind that even a legitimate use may be seen by some as dishonest and, depending on your social standing or position, you may want to avoid even the appearance of fraud. Remember also that a nominee is your agent. Although you may include damage clauses in your agreement for inappropriate action by him, in all likelihood you remain the responsible party with regard to those parties damaged by your nominee's action.

An accountant should know how to handle transactions involving income that appears to be the nominee's but is actually the Principle's. The IRS has forms including the 1099 to pass that income responsibility on.

For those that hoped this chapter would include samples of the types of contracts discussed as well as some Partnership and LLC agreements, I have provided several sample contracts in Appendix C.

CHAPTER 11

Uniform Commercial Code

The "Uniform Commercial Code," or "UCC," is basically the codification in the United States and elsewhere of what is referred to internationally as the "Law Merchant" or "Merchant Law." Like those for statutory entities, there are basic rules governing commerce between companies, states, and even nations. These rules apply to the sale of merchandise, contracts, delivery of goods, shipping and receiving, and which party or parties are responsible at each point in a transaction. Included are procedures for Invoicing, Bills of Lading, and Insurance as well as rules for Negotiable Instruments and their Acceptance, Honor, Dishonor, and Discharge.

Just as with those statutes governing artificial statutory entities, the UCC take precedence over terms and procedures not otherwise written or agreed to between parties. As an example, you Invoice (bill) another company for goods previously sold and shipped to them, they pay late or fail to pay, and you are forced to bring suit to collect. If your original Invoice did not declare an interest penalty for late payment, none will be collectible. However, if your Packing Slip and Invoices declare an interest rate for late payment or cost of collection, if necessary, these amounts may be awarded. This is because the customer's previous acceptance of the goods is considered an acceptance of the terms on your Invoices.

Whole books can and have been written on this topic alone. My purpose here is to simply call your attention to the fact that if your business involves more than point-of-sale purchases, you may have certain issues to consider. As another example, you sell a heavy piece of equipment to a company some distance from you. When is the equipment considered to belong to the customer? After he pays for it but while it still sits in your place of business? Or after you put it on a truck to have it delivered? When the truck leaves your place of business does the equipment then belong to the customer or not until it gets there in good condition? If an accident occurs in route, you may claim it as fine when it left your hands. But your customer may claim he never received it, so you still owe him what he bought.

As you can see from this example, not having shared expectations with the customer or being ignorant of standard practices could leave you with unexpected losses and obligations. If it's clear to the customer that it is his equipment the minute it leaves your dock, then he will be sure to take responsibility for its being insured from that point. If, on the other hand, it has been agreed that you will deliver it safely to his place, then said insurance or risk is on you. The examples presented should make it clear how important your Forms, Paperwork, and Agreements are to reducing risk, misunderstanding, lawsuits, and loss.

By looking for the Uniform Commercial Code on the business websites of most SOSs, you will find a Registration System for Debtors and Creditors. By filing a UCC-1 Form, a Creditor can name a Debtor and give Public Notice of Security Agreements. In much the same way, a bank will record a mortgage with the County Recorder against Real Estate, or place a Lien on the Title of your vehicle with the Registry of Motor Vehicles. Similarly, any other Creditor can put a Lien and Public Notice against an individual or a company's Assets.

Although most large equipment such as milling machines, lathes, or even bulldozers and tractors have serial numbers, models, and makes, there is no central place of registration for these and other Business Assets. Therefore, when such Assets are sold on credit or placed as collateral, the UCC-1 Form is documented and registered to show the Security Interest one individual or company has in another. It serves as Public Notice to all others that their claim against the same Debtor may be unsecured or subordinate to the earlier claim. Therefore, as a Creditor, it is important to use this Registry to establish the priority of your claim or to recognize that your extension of credit will not be superior. As a Debtor, it is important to be sure Creditors release their claim once the debt has been paid. Filings are usually posted for a set period such as five years. If your Debtors still owe, you should be sure and renew your claim or notice of it will drop off. Likewise, Debtors need to be sure if their debt is cleared to have it released. Otherwise, it may cause a delay if you seek Credit elsewhere and the new Creditor believes they are subordinate to another claim. In some instances, a new Creditor may ask you to convince a previous Creditor to subordinate their claim to receive the new Credit.

In any case, it should be noted—we have all heard the caveat "Buyer Beware"—that if you are considering buying machinery, heavy equipment, or other Business Assets from an individual or a business, it is your responsibility to check the Registry for Liens. Should you make a large purchase of such items and fail to do so, you may be surprised to find that a Registered Creditor (Lienholder) may take back his collateral (the machine you bought), leaving you an unsecured Creditor chasing the person you purchased from for satisfaction. And you have also probably heard the old saying, "You can't get blood from a stone." Or, like the Rolling Stones' hit song, "I Can't Get No (Satisfaction)."

Another scenario you should be careful of when borrowing money from a bank or Lease Company, for instance, for a piece of equipment, is the wording on the claim. You may have no choice if you want the loan but to allow a UCC-1 filing against the equipment you are purchasing. However, ensure that along with listing the Serial Number and description of the equipment, the lender has not made broad general statements regarding other equipment and assets you own already, or such things as receivables, future income, etc. Otherwise, they will have the first claim on all of it. This could affect decisions that will be made by others regarding your future credit, while the lender's debt remains outstanding.

While on the topic of Creditors and Debtors, it should be noted that when your company lends or borrows, it has the potential of being both of these. If you Invoice customers and allow payment after the fact, by any span of time, your business is a Creditor and your customer a Debtor. At the same time, if you are allowed to pay your bills after receiving them, you are a Debtor to your vendors. Always be mindful of the fact that when you allow Debtors to owe you, you are either extending or lending them your own equity or savings or re-lending them that which has been loaned to you. For example, let's say that you own a machine company that produces a product made from brass. The supplier of brass bars that you use to make your products allows you to buy as much as $20,000 worth at a time. This means you have a $20,000 Credit line with them. You sell this brass product to your customers and allow them 30 days to pay the Invoice you send them. Then, depending on their number and the amount you extend to each is, in essence, the amount of the Credit line you have with your brass supplier that you are passing on to others. Therefore, extreme care should be taken to consider the number and amount of Open Accounts you allow your customers so as to prevent any one or more of them from affecting your company's Credit. For example, allowing each of 20 different customers a $500 Credit line would be a risk of 50% of your credit line. But considering the chance that 20 different customers will all become slow or non-payers all at once is very minute, hence not very risky. However, should you allow only a couple of customers a $5,000 Credit line, the risk becomes much greater and any one or more could seriously affect your ability to pay your Creditor.

The bottom line is that having customers larger and more creditworthy than your own company does not put you or your business in a position to extend credit beyond your means. The previous examples are simplified to make a point. Although a company may have multiple sources of credit from banks, vendors, lease companies, etc., any company with large Accounts Receivable (outstanding invoices) needs to keep an eye on their overdue accounts. Realize that every dollar of interest on borrowed funds, equal to the amount of overdue funds owed you, is interest you are paying on behalf of others—in other words, *lost profits.*

Many small companies and even large ones sometimes use their existing inventory of product and supplies, or their receivables (outstanding Invoices not yet paid), to borrow money to keep operations running. These techniques can be very beneficial to the rapidly growing company with restricted Capital or cash flow. It can allow a small company to fill a huge order they might otherwise need to pass on and help add important new customers and business to their market share.

You may hear these described as Receivable and Inventory financing (loan) or Factoring Receivables. Usually, a company pledges inventory, assets, and outstanding invoicing as collateral for loans against a certain percentage of the outstanding receivable or existing inventory. Payments are scheduled and maintained against a ratio of the outstanding invoices actually loaned against. Payments can increase if your customers become slower at paying you back within terms. For instance, you have a huge order that just came in and need to buy the materials to make your product and make the sale. So you take Invoices that you have already sent to customers who owe you, say $20,000, and should pay within 30 days. This $20,000 of invoices is pledged to the Factoring Company (Private Lender) who agrees to lend you up to 75% of the outstanding Invoices (your receivables). In this case that comes to $15,000 for a 2% discount of the invoices, with a .25% per-day penalty for invoices over 30 days old.

So you take your $15,000 advance against your invoices and use it to buy raw materials and to meet other costs associated with filling your new order, thereby creating yet more invoicing.

If 80% of the Invoice you pledged is paid within the 30-day term and, say, the other 20% takes an extra month to collect, you will pay the Factoring Company (Lender) a total of $700. This is 2% of the pledged Invoices ($20,000) or $400 plus .25% per day on the late 20% portion of the Invoices (4,000 x .0025 x 30 days), or $300, for a total of $700 on loan. If you continue to borrow against the ongoing invoice at the same average amount and rate, that constant outstanding balance of $15,000 annualized would cost the company $4,000 in interest for the year. The Factoring Company would be producing a 28% rate of return on its Capital lending for its investors.

This is a great moneymaker for the lender and an acceptable deal or necessary evil for the rapidly growing small business in need of Capital. However, it is an absolute death knell for any small business that selects these methods to overcome financial problems, slow business, or overextended credit to slow-paying customers.

If the only way you can create or increase business is by extending credit and payment terms, you need to take a hard look at your pricing or the actual viability of your business model. Let's assume you have a good and desirable product or service but do not have the Capital or size to open accounts. A solution is to let those customers claiming to have excellent credit—for which you should be willing to extend terms—get a loan, use Visa or MasterCard, or obtain a "Letter of Credit" from their bank.

For instance, let's say you have a high-priced product or service you do not want to release or perform until payment is received. But the customer does not wish to make payment until they receive the product or service and determine it to be genuine or as described. The reluctance on each side can be satisfied with a Letter of Credit. This is a situation that takes place often with international transactions. No U.S. manufacturer, for instance, wants to ship costly goods or materials overseas and hope to be paid once they get there. Nor does the overseas customer wish to make payment to a Company here and then find the goods were never sent. The cost of going to and then dealing with an unknown legal system of the other jurisdiction in an attempt to get satisfaction is prohibitive. One bad transaction could eliminate the profit of many good transactions.

These risks may be overcome or significantly reduced by the use of a Letter of Credit. If a customer in the foreign location is indeed trustworthy and creditworthy, he can place funds with or be extended credit by his own bank. In turn, the bank will send a Letter of Credit expressing its willingness to pay the invoice irrevocably, upon the meeting of certain conditions by the seller. This promise is made to the seller's bank by the buyer's bank. The conditions usually include Shipping Manifests showing goods shipped and quantities from one point and their subsequent arrival on Bills of Lading at the arriving point. At this time, funds are released bank to bank. Some quality control or other criteria may also be involved depending on the particulars in various industries or service sectors.

As stated previously, this chapter is not meant to be a comprehensive discussion on UCC law or the topics associated with it. It is intended only to introduce the UCC to the new small business owner along with some considerations and issues on which he may need to seek out more knowledge.

CHAPTER 12

Insurance

The use of "Insurance" to combat the risk of loss is prevalent not only in our personal lives but equally, if not more so, in the business world. Added to the list of health, life, vehicle, and building insurance are Workers Compensation, General Liability, Product Liability, Key Man Coverage, Inventory Loss Protection, Data Loss, and more.

Except for certain life insurance policies, insurance coverage on and for your business, assets, and employees are deductible expenses and part of the cost of doing business. Particular types of insurance are optional for some businesses; their cost should be weighed against the likelihood of specific occurrences. Other kinds are desirable to have and can be used to attract high-quality personnel. Still others, such as General Liability, may be required for some companies to do business. Finally, some businesses are mandated by law to carry Workers Compensation insurance, while others that are a certain size or that have a certain number of employees must carry Health Insurance.

As mentioned in Chapter 12, most states require you to have Workers Compensation as soon as you hire your first employee. I do not recommend going even one day without this coverage; it should be in place before you hire any personnel. If you use leased or secured temporary labor from a company designed for such purposes, such as Kelly Girls, Office Temps or Work Force, they should provide this coverage for these workers. But you would be wise to require them to send you an Insurance Binder as proof. Their insurance company should have no problem faxing or otherwise providing a copy of a one-page document naming your company as an additional insured under the lease company's Workers Compensation Plan. This coverage pays medical expenses and a portion of lost wages to any employee unable to work for any length of time as a result of a work-related injury.

Another mandated insurance coverage for some companies in some states, usually depending on the number of total employees and their hours worked, is Health Insurance coverage. The mandated types and amounts also vary. This type of insurance may also be provided by some companies, whether mandated or not, as a means of attracting skilled or otherwise desirable employees. Many factors go into the selection of these plans.

Along with cost, companies must also decide whether an employee will be required to contribute to their coverage and whether to offer family plans. Should the policy cover all costs or have co-payments or deductibles? A high-deductible plan with only catastrophic coverage, or low-deductible comprehensive coverage? Small close-knit family-run companies may opt for complete coverage, even at a higher cost, as an indirect way of providing higher pay with tax savings to both the business and the individuals. Health insurance is a fully deductible expense for the company and, as a fringe benefit to the employee, is not considered an increase in salary. It should be noted that a business is not allowed to discriminate, so such benefits cannot be offered to some employees, for example, family members or friends, and not others.

Vehicle insurance is another often-mandated coverage and, if not done so by the state, is usually still required by the lease company or lender, if any. Vehicles are high-liability assets and therefore warrant insurance for that fact alone, as well as a means of a replacement for the cost of damaged equipment or injury to people.

General Liability insurance, although rarely mandated by law for most industries, is sometimes required by other businesses, customers, and lenders for them to want to do business with you. For instance, a General Contractor of a large construction project may not be willing to hire your small framing company as a subcontractor if you do not have certain minimum coverages. Or a homeowner hiring your company to make an addition or repair a roof may want to hire only an insured contractor. Your General Liability policy, often a company's initial general business coverage with an insurance company, may cover your damaging others accidentally by your service or products. Fire, theft, and other damage to your buildings, inventory, or other assets may be added to it. The cost of this coverage depends on coverage amounts desired combined with annual sales amounts and other factors.

Key Man Coverage is Life Insurance; instead of protecting the wife and children of a company employee or owner for his untimely death, it protects the company. Hence the name Key Man. If, for instance, time, effort, and capital have been invested in a business idea, invention, product, or venture that is heavily dependent upon the expertise, knowledge, and abilities of one or more key individuals, it may be desirable to insure them. Therefore, if they were to die and be unavailable to continue, said investment could be recouped or the business could otherwise be sustained until replacement. Partners may obtain this kind of coverage on each other to provide for the business upset caused by such an occurrence.

Let me give my opinion regarding the options available for Key Man Coverage, which, as stated, is Life Insurance. Term insurance coverage of some fixed-level premium, such as a 10- or 20-year level term, is the only coverage worth considering. The very first term insurance products offered were annual renewable term, and this coverage became increasingly more expensive with age. This fact would be used by most insurance agents to discourage the purchase of term insurance in favor of the other option, Whole Life insurance. Whole Life insurance would be touted as the way to go; it is slightly more expensive at first, but premiums remain the same for life. In addition to this so-called great feature (the same price for life), it is also touted as a private savings account (cash value) within the policy—one you could even borrow from if you ever needed to. My opinion, in a word, Baloney!

What they fail to tell you is that you overpay for insurance, the same overpayment all of your life. If you borrow from your so-called "savings," the amount is deducted from the death benefit if death occurs. This means your family gets paid your savings as part of the death benefit. These companies that have built large marble, glass, and ivory towers in every city have done young families a gross disservice.

Imagine as a young man with a wife and two children you get talked into paying, say, $600 a year for a $50,000 Life

Insurance benefit with a so-called "savings plan" attached. You're young, have no savings, are saddled with a mortgage and a car payment, and you die. The insurance company pays your wife $50,000. She pays for your burial, pays off the car and other bills, and has a few thousand left to live on until she can find a job and attempt to keep the mortgage paid and the children fed. She later finds out that $350 a year could have bought a term policy on you for $250,000 or more in coverage, and that the $250 per year saved could have been in a real investment and gained interest. This death benefit would have paid all the bills, the car, and the whole mortgage. Or it could have been placed in interest in funds earning $20,000 to $25,000 annually perpetually. "Oh, but what if I didn't die and the insurance cost got prohibitively high as I got older," you ask? I say, "So what?" By then the children are grown, the mortgage is paid, and the difference was invested. Drop the insurance. You don't need it now.

Today things are even better, and term insurance has far more options than annual renewable—at 5-, 10-, and even 20-year-level premiums. High death benefit, low-cost insurance, no gimmicks. Simply compare a $500,000 death benefit for a term of 20 years with Company A against the same at Company B. Investing and insurance are two different things. There is only one reason to combine them, and that is to confuse you about how much the insurance costs and how much is being saved at what rate of interest. I don't care if it's Whole Life, Variable Life, or Universal Life. It's all a scheme for insurance companies to make higher commissions in those ivory-tower buildings.

If you're reading this book and your brother-in-law has sold you that crap, I am sure he will cuss me out and call up my limited knowledge of insurance products and how the tax-free death benefit proceeds and future annuity options can dovetail to your tax advantage blah, blah, bull. I'll leave it at that. Ultimately, it's a decision you make for yourself and your family.

Insurance is about asset protection and, earlier in this chapter, I made mention of vehicles being high-liability assets. So let me talk here briefly about asset types. Later, after I describe individually the various entities such as Partnerships, Corporations, etc., I will explain entity interactions and make some suggestions. The adage about not putting all your eggs in one basket will come up, and these asset types should be kept in mind. Insurance can protect you from a loss, but it can also make you an appealing target by the "looking for something for nothing" crowd. Realizing this can help you arrange the assets in your various baskets wisely.

There are what I call high-, low-, and neutral-liability assets. Among the high would be such things as vehicles—you could drive downtown today and have an accident for which you may be at fault or at least become involved in an argument claiming that you are. A low-liability asset would be Real Estate, which, although not immune from suit, is less likely to be the cause of one as opposed to a vehicle. Neutral-liability assets might include bank accounts, bonds, etc.—someone may want your money in the bank, but it is unlikely to be the cause of an action. So, short of further explanation later, I would suggest that it may be unwise to place vehicles (high-liability assets) in the same basket as Real Estate (low-liability asset) or high-balance bank accounts or investments.

CHAPTER 13

Trusts and Foundations

A "Trust" is a contract that includes certain terms that establish a "Fiduciary" responsibility, for at least one party toward another. One party delivers income and or assets to another party to conserve, manage, distribute, or dispose of for the benefit of yet a third party or parties.

All Trusts have some combination of the following attributes. They are "Revocable" or "Irrevocable," "Living" (Inter-Vivos) or "Testamentary" (after death [Will]), and "Statutory" or "Non-Statutory." Revocable means that a person can revoke or change their mind about what was placed in Trust. Irrevocable means a person cannot revoke or change their mind about the Trust terms or property after the agreement has been entered into. A Living Trust, sometimes referred to by attorneys as Inter-Vivos (a Latin term for "While Living"), is a trust whose terms go into effect during the Grantor's lifetime. Testamentary, on the other hand, is when the Trust terms are activated by the death of the "Testator" or Grantor, such as with a Will. Statutory versus Non-Statutory, which was discussed in previous chapters on different entities, applies to Trusts as well.

There are many types of both Statutory and Non-Statutory Trusts—too many to list here. Some very common ones are known simply by the Titles of their main attributes. One such Trust that many have heard of is the Living Trust. Although there are many types of Living Trusts, often when someone says they have a Living Trust they are referring to a Statutory, Revocable, Living Trust designed by an attorney for a married couple to pass their estate on to their children. You may also hear of this type as an AB Living Trust. The AB refers to the husband and wife and describes terms pertinent to one spouse dying before the other, making the living spouse the first beneficiary before any remainder of assets goes to the children. This type of Trust, when properly written and executed, can serve to bypass probate. Although this Trust type may serve a limited purpose well, it does not provide great asset protection. And when executed incorrectly it can be totally useless.

It should be stated here that, like doctors, lawyers have various specialties. You wouldn't go to a general practitioner to remove a brain tumor. Likewise, many attorneys do not know anything more than you will know after reading this chapter— and some even less. A competent lawyer is worth the fee and can save you money and headaches in the long run. But a lazy, incompetent one who puts a CD in his computer and selects a prewritten form to print may cost you plenty of both.

Before getting more into the Trust contract itself, I take this time to write about attorneys. My number one pet peeve is when they do their clients the type of disservice I have seen over and over again in my years dealing with Trusts. Most couples I advise admit to having little knowledge of the topic. Occasionally, however, I will get one that says, "Oh yes! We have a Trust." I usually ask to see it, and in way too many instances find that it is a typical Living or AB Living Trust.

Usually, they say they heard of someone else who had one, so they asked their attorney about it. The attorney replies, "Oh, if you want a trust, we can do that. I'll draw it up and call you to come in and sign it." Then a few weeks later they show up to the attorney's office, sign their new trust, and take it home and place it in their strongbox with other important papers. Then they receive a bill from the attorney from anywhere between $3,000 and $5,000 for his work. This Trust usually states that Mr. and Mrs. Smith, for example, the "Grantors," grant to Mr. and Mrs. Smith as "Trustees" (themselves) the Smith Family Trust for the benefit of Mr. and Mrs. Smith, the first "Beneficiaries," and secondly to the children Tom Smith (son) and Becky Smith-Jones (daughter) upon the death of their parents, etc. I then ask, "What did you place in the Trust?" At this point they usually look mystified and say, "You know, the house, all our stuff, I don't know." So we go on to check the Deed and bank accounts, etc., usually finding that nothing has been placed into this so-called "Trust." Now, this is what I call malpractice and a travesty. Not only is this not a bona-fide Trust, but nothing has been put into it so nothing will bypass probate and you will still need an attorney when probate occurs.

The trust described is actually just an alter ego. The couple is using an alternative name—in this case, The Smith Family Trust—instead of their own names. Now, if assets such as the home had actually been deeded to it, it would have at least served as a Revocable Living Trust and bypassed probate court despite not technically meeting the definition of a Trust.

A document whereby the Smiths as Grantors granted the property to Trustees other than themselves for the benefit of their children would be a bona-fide Trust arrangement, unlike what was done. If you give something away to yourself, it is not a Trust. In the Smith case, had an asset been included in the transaction the Title of the asset would have changed from that of Mr. or Mrs. Smith to that of the Smith Family Trust. But no real change in ownership would have occurred, hence, the Trust is just an alter ego.

Let's move on to the positions or roles of the actual parties to a Trust to make things clearer. We normally have the person(s) who are placing assets such as money, businesses, income streams, or other property into the Trust. This party is most often referred to as the Grantor or, if more than one such as husband and wife, the Grantors. This position may also be called Settlor, Dedicator, or Exchanger. In the case of a Will, which is technically a Testamentary Trust, it may be Testator or Decedent. The Grantor is the person who usually called for or sought the arrangement in order to place certain valuable assets into the Trust. Although in some Trusts additional grants or donations of assets may occur at a later time or by additional parties, the Grantor often makes the original—if not all—grant of assets. Therefore, in most cases, the Trust terms found in the Trust Contract or Indenture are designed to meet the wishes of the Grantor. After all, the person giving away the assets usually wants to see how the funds are used, who shall receive them, or both. The intentions of the Grantor and whether they want the option to change their mind or the terms of the Trust in the future will depend on whether they want it to be Revocable or Irrevocable.

A Revocable Trust requires less certainty or less trust since the Grantor can change his mind about it at a later date. Of course, for the same reason, it provides less asset protection. An Irrevocable Trust provides much better asset protection precisely because it cannot be undone. This, however, also requires more certainty and more faith. For this reason, many more people talk about Trusts than actually form them because when it comes right down to it, few people are really that trusting and prefer to keep full control. A real bona-fide Trust requires just that—trust—in someone else. Hence you find Trusts similar to the one previously described in this chapter, where little faith is required and an alter ego is established rather than a bona-fide Trust.

Another position in the Trust Organization is the Trustee. The Trustee is the person usually selected by the Grantor of the Trust. He or she should be a person of good character in whom the Grantor has faith. The Trustee agrees to be bound by the Trust Indenture (its contract) and is willing to carry out the wishes of the Grantor as written in the terms of the Agreement. A Trust may have one or more Trustees depending on the terms of the Agreement. It may have several who act as a Board of Trustees.

Depending on the contract, the Grantor may select the first or all Trustees immediately. It may be that the first Trustee has authority to choose another or several as the management needs of the Trust come to dictate. It is a good idea to make sure that terms are included that state how a Trustee is to be added or removed should the need arise. In the case of a single Trustee, having a Successor Trustee at the ready in case of death, disability, or incapacity is also wise. A Trustee takes on a fiduciary role, meaning a position of trust and responsibility. He oversees the holding, managing, and distribution of the

Trust's property, investments, and/or other assets. He does this not for his own benefit but for the best interest of the beneficiaries of the Trust. In fact, to act only in his own interest would be a breach of fiduciary responsibility, which can carry heavy legal penalties in most jurisdictions.

Some Agreements allow the Trustee very broad powers to make almost any decision he thinks best for the Trust and its beneficiaries. Other contracts may limit the Trustee to very few decision options and require all actions to be predetermined, with little leeway for changes or discretion. Some may even require the beneficiary's permission or agreement, while others leave the beneficiary no say at all. The beauty of Trusts is they are just contracts articulating the wishes of the Trust founders. The better the articulation of and foresight into the terms of the Trust Agreement, the less room for controversy between the parties of the contract and the better the chance that the Grantor or founder will have their wishes and visions carried out as planned. Other names or titles that may be used to denote the fiduciary position besides Trustee might be Steward, Conservator, Executor, or Receiver. It's important to choose an individual you can trust to carry out your wishes or the terms of the Agreement. But it should also be noted that if you are creating an Irrevocable Trust and desire the attribute of strong asset protection, you should consider a person "at arm's length." This refers to an individual who is seen by others (namely, the courts) as being someone you do not control. For instance, choosing a relative such as your child, sibling, or parent—or even an employee of a company you own—who depends on you for continued employment may not be considered to be "at arm's length." But choosing such a person does not make the Trust illegal or invalid; it simply means that the so-called "Irrevocability" or absence of control may be questioned if a lawsuit or controversy arises in the future.

It is understandable that you may trust someone close or related to you over others, but selecting someone who seems to be under your control may weaken your asset protection plan. A compromise or middle-of-the road solution may be to choose more than one Trustee: one who is very close to you who you are confident will carry out your wishes as expressed in the Trust Agreement, and another "at arm's length" such as an attorney or accountant who can see to the legal aspects of the Agreement and the Trust Corpus.

The third position or role in the Trust is that of the Beneficiary or, if more than one, the Beneficiaries. The Beneficiary is the person or persons who benefit from the Trust. They are typically the reason the Grantor established a Trust in the first place. Beneficiaries may also be called Beneficial Interest Holders, Certificate Holders, or Heirs depending on the Trust language or type. When there are multiple Beneficiaries, income or assets may be split equally, by various percentages, or even by specific assets. These are all decisions to be made by the Grantors and articulated in the Trust Agreement. Beneficial Interest may even follow a preferential order, for instance, by making one or more persons First-Tier and other persons Second- or even Third-Tier Beneficiaries. In this manner, a husband may leave all his property to his wife and children in one Trust by designating his wife First-Tier Beneficiary and his children Second-Tier. This could have the effect of leaving everything to the benefit of the wife while she is alive and then passing the remainder to the children at her death.

As described concerning the Trustees, the Beneficiary can be given the power to approve or disapprove actions by the Trustee. He may be able to make requests for distribution from the Trust or, depending on the Trust's design, have little or even no say at all over the Trustee or distributions.

Trusts can and have been formed for more reasons than this book can contain. A few examples might include grandparents placing funds in Trust to send their grandchildren to college, causing a particular property to pass from generation to generation, or leaving funds to provide for a physically or mentally disabled family member.

A Trust may provide for the distribution of all its assets to a particular individual at the time of the death of another, or it may provide for the preservation of an investment or assets for a period of time or until the Beneficiary attains a certain age. Alternatively, a Trust may provide for the Beneficiaries from the income generated by its assets but not distribute the assets or principle corpus of the Trust itself.

Land Trusts can be set up to hold property. Real Estate Investment Trusts are established by investors to benefit from the profits of professionals managing, buying, and selling Real Estate. Irrevocable Life Insurance Trusts can be created to hold Life Insurance policies on entire families to establish a Family Dynasty. Pure Trusts, Contract Trusts, and Business Trusts can be formed to hold and run businesses as unincorporated business organizations, sometimes called UBOs.

There is no end to the type and reasons for Trusts. The Foundation is another fancy term for a Trust Organization. It is often formed for a particular purpose, cause, or ideal having a broader or more general class of beneficiaries such as the public at large, humankind in general, or some more specific segment such as crime victims, the disabled, sufferers of cancer or black lung, or numerous others. Foundations may conduct research for science, medicine, or astronomy. They might be formed for political ideals, religious endeavors, or the saving of the environment or the whale.

The above description of Foundations may sound similar to what many refer to as 501c3 Corporations, which are formed for charitable, scientific, or educational purposes. And indeed they are, except that 501c3 organizations can be Corporations and any community chest, fund, or foundation that has filed for the status of a 501c3 organization by making an application to the IRS. Foundations that desire to be considered tax-exempt must also apply under section 501c3, just as many other entity types. The only exception to this rule is the 508c3, for the Church (Christian), which need not make the application. Those Foundations and Trusts that do not apply are usually considered Private Foundations. There are many nuances regarding Charitable Trusts, Foundations, and Feeder Organizations, etc. that have various tax issues about which I suggest you seek out professional help or advice.

The Unincorporated Business Organization (UBO) and Pure Trust Organization (PTO) were once a popular format for business formations among wealthy Capitalists. Their popularity is again on the rise, only now that popularity has arisen among certain groups—typically less wealthy but historically knowledgeable individuals such as Patriots, Free State advocates, and other Constitutional-minded people. With that increase has also come much misinformation regarding such business formations. The most significant part of this misinformation and error has to do with taxation and/or the supposed lack thereof. Please review my warnings regarding these business types near the end of Chapter 7!

There is nothing illegal or unlawful about doing business in a Trust arrangement of this type. The bad press regarding a Pure Trust Organization has come about because of the ignorance of many of the promoters selling wording for these Trust Indentures. They don't know the difference between a taxable entity and a taxable transaction. Please read my warnings in Chapter 7 and seek proper advice. Seek the truth, not what you wish the truth were.

Due to the stigma developing against the Pure Trust, you may be introduced to it or a similar type of entity by names such as Constitutional Trust, Contract Trust, Business Trust, Freedom Trust, etc. The typical format of these entities is one in which Business Assets are granted to or exchanged by the Grantors or Exchangers and placed into the Trust or Business Organization, to be run and managed by Trustees or Managing Directors. In exchange for the granted assets, Certificates are given to the Exchangers representative of their share of the business. These are shares of Beneficial Interest, and they may be retained by the Exchanger who becomes a Beneficial Certificate Holder, sort of like a stockholder in an incorporated business.

As stated, these organizations can be a great vehicle with which to conduct business. They are typically Non-Statutory and can change venue with little hassle. Their Trustees and Managers usually have full control and considerable latitude for quick, unencumbered decision making. Certificate Holders typically have little to no say in business operations and receive only profit or loss when distributions are made by the Trustees. The Certificate Holder's actual interest is in the Trust's Estate, not in any current or actual Business Assets or property. Although the Trustees have considerable latitude in their actions, technically they do have a fiduciary responsibility to the Beneficial Interest Holders.

The confusion regarding taxation is understandable given the complicated tax code within the United States. Due to the numerous types of Trusts and Business Types, it is sometimes difficult to ascertain whose advice to follow. Certainly, many attorneys and accountants never deal with these types of entities and may know little regarding them. That said, seeking the advice of an attorney or accountant who at least claims to know is far superior to your listening to the guy who sold you a copy of Business Trust wording and insists there are no taxes.

Statutory Trusts usually file a Form 1041. Whether a Trust is Simple or Complex will affect the Trust's taxes. Simple Trusts call for income to be distributed annually. Complex Trusts, well, they're more complex. In simple terms, a Trust that passes all its income through annually to the Beneficiaries will have little to no tax due, very similar to a Partnership filing. A K1 will be issued to the IRS and the Beneficiaries reporting the income distributed to each Beneficiary. A Trust that retains its income will be taxed at a relatively high rate. This is to discourage individuals from hiding personal income within Trusts; although this may help with privacy issues, you will pay a tax in the amount of if not greater than that shown personally.

Non-Statutory Trusts, as well as some simple Grantor Trusts, may have no filing requirement at all. These are referred to as "Disregarded" or "Disregarded Entities" by the

IRS. This is where much of the confusion within the tax freedom, Patriot, or sovereignty movements comes in. Reading such statements in the tax code or the Court's publishings regarding disregarded and non-tax entities, these movements believe they have discovered secrets the government doesn't want you to know. Passing on erroneous law theories have gotten many well-meaning individuals into a lot of trouble and caused much suffering and loss.

"Disregarded" means the IRS does not recognize or individually regulate such entities, but instead looks to the individuals involved and the substance of the transactions they are involved in. The IRS expects the individual to claim any taxable income on taxable transactions on their personal returns. It does not mean that income within, run through, or associated with the Disregarded Entity is non-taxable. Remember, taxable or non-taxable income has to do with sources of income from within or without the "United States" and your status as a U.S. citizen, person, alien, or native and being a resident or non-resident.

Trustees of Business Trusts that may otherwise be considered a Disregarded Entity may consider voluntary filing under the rules for an Association or Partnership. By filing a 1026 Partnership Return for a Contract Trust or UBO, you can avoid the stigma of the tax movement arguments and still maintain a non-taxable entity since a Partnership filing is for a pass-through entity. The Trust itself will have no tax liability. Responsibility for tax liabilities will be averted by allowing the various individuals transacting with the Trust and receiving distributions to be responsible for their own tax liabilities and decisions regarding their status, reporting, and payment.

More popular than using a Trust as a business entity is the use of Trusts for holding and passing personal property, money, and Real Estate. As stated previously, whether you use a Revocable or Irrevocable Trust and whether you pass title now or after death are individual choices based on your goals and plans and your sureness regarding them. You may plan to leave your savings and your home to your children, but while these assets remain in your possession or titled to you personally, they are part of your wealth and your estate. Should debt, lawsuit, medical care, or bankruptcy occur or result in a judgment against you, your assets may be taken to satisfy said judgment or debt. One method of avoiding such an occurrence is to settle an Irrevocable Trust before such an event occurs.

If you have already given your ownership interest in a business, financial account, or Real Estate prior to anyone having a claim against you, then those assets will no longer be yours to lose. Once a judgment occurs or, in some cases, even after you become aware of the likelihood that one may occur or that someone is planning a claim against you, it may be too late. It may even be considered a fraudulent conveyance. Early planning is much better and easier than emergency planning. You cannot foresee the time and date of accidents, ill health, death, or disability but you can incorporate contingencies ahead of time as part of contract writing and business and Estate Planning as you go.

Many people I meet with are surprised to find that they can put their home in Trust even if they still have a mortgage on it. In the early days of home mortgages, most loans were assumable. This meant that if you could no longer pay your loan, you could contract with or find someone to take your property and make payments for you. After a great inflation period in the '70s during which this occurred frequently, bankers began refining their mortgage contracts, and today every mortgage has removed the assumable language and now has what is called a "due on sale clause" written within it. This prevents the transfer of property and lower interest rates being passed from one party to another prior to the bank's mortgage being paid in full. This makes it possible for the bank to review and take a new application from the next prospective owner of the property. However, in October 1982 the Garn-St Germain Depository Institutions Act was passed by Congress. One aspect of this legislation prevents banks from exercising their "due on sale clause" under certain circumstances, among which include certain Estate Planning considerations. Banks are prohibited from using the transfer of Title into Trust for the benefit of certain relations such as husband, wife, children, mother, father, etc. without a change of occupancy and so forth as an excuse to call the loan even though transfer occurs.

Some people are under the impression that if they place their property in a Trust, they have some ironclad container that cannot be touched or sued. Although this impression comes from certain truths, it is mostly fiction. The fact is anyone can bring suit against almost anyone else just by making an accusation or demand and then filing a claim. The reason why property in a trust may be safer is because, done right, the property is no longer yours. Therefore, if you are sued, the Trust that is not yours should not be included since it is not part of your estate and the claimant may not have standing against it. Secondly, a Trust being an artificial person does not walk, talk, or drive and therefore have accidents, or insult or damage other people, so there are fewer reasons to name it in a lawsuit. Lastly, the aspect of split title and rights among the various parties within the Trust arrangement give judges pause not to damage innocent or uninvolved parties to satisfy a judgment against a single party. In an Irrevocable Trust, for instance, the property was once the Grantor's but is no longer his; it is now with the Trustee. However, it is not the Trustee's, as he holds it for the benefit of someone else, the Beneficiary, and yet it is not the Beneficiary's as he has not yet received the property. Therefore, to make a judgment against the Trust property because of a claim against any one of the individuals involved—the Grantor, Trustee, or Beneficiary— would be to inadvertently cause damage to the other two parties. This would give rise to a claim by each of them for their losses against the party responsible for that decision.

So a Trust that does business with the public—for example, owns a poorly maintained building in which someone is hurt— may be sued as can any person at law. However, a Trust that is a container for a property is certainly less likely to be named in one than are most individuals.

There is certainly more information, nuances, types, and circumstances regarding Trusts and their uses than I can include in a single chapter of this book. Hopefully, this chapter has added to your basic understanding about Trusts and aided your ability to articulate to a professional of your choice any desire you may have to form one.

CHAPTER 14

Pick Your Entity Type and Plan

Now that you have read about each of the various entity types, you are getting closer to deciding which one you want to use to do business. In this chapter, I will ask questions, offer more food for thought, and even repeat information from previous chapters for reinforcement and retention.

Many people often wait until they are old enough that the prospect of dying is unavoidable before they will write a will or otherwise do Estate Planning. In my opinion, this is a mistake. The unforeseen happens more often than you might think, albeit always to someone else—or at least we hope. As soon as you accumulate assets, whether business, financial accounts, or Real Estate, you should have a plan for transferring them to someone else.

Your business plan should be laid out with an eye on its transition to your Estate Plan. If something happens to you after you successfully establish a business, who do you want to run it? Who do you want to own it? Are these the same? Or do you want it sold and the value given to your heirs? Immediately or later? Would that require a Trust or a Will? You're not sure you can answer all those questions, right? It's true that the answer to some of them are very dependent on the future. For that reason, most people wait to weigh these matters. Yet the key to overcoming this problem is not looking to the future but answering the questions as you would today. It doesn't matter if you are young and hope to eventually have four children to whom you will leave your business. If it had to be done today, what would the answer be? Apply that answer now and make the appropriate changes if and when "later" gets here. The beauty of contracts, agreements, and businesses is that—just like people—they can be changed to accommodate different directions and goals. But by answering the questions as you would today, you can have things in place should they arrive sooner than expected.

Even a young person just over the age of majority who has not yet acquired any substantial assets can, with four simple legal documents, put an Estate Plan in place for little to no cost that will serve them until some amount of assets have been accumulated, or business success comes to fruition. These items include a Living Will, "Pour-Over" Will, Power-of-Attorney, and simple Trust.

First, a Living Will—sometimes called a Health Care Proxy—should state your basic wishes for extraordinary care or the lack thereof and name the person who will make your medical choices should you be unable to do so for yourself. Second, what I call a Pour-Over Will is actually just a regular Will. I call it this because I am not a fan of the Will itself or at least not as it is typically used. More on that in a moment. This Pour-Over Will would name desired guardians of your children, if any, and the disposition of any sudden, unexpected wealth such as a recent or pending inheritance, lottery winnings, or other assets not yet properly directed or accounted for in existing Trusts or Businesses. Third is the Power-of-

Attorney, which you may give to a very trusted friend, relative, or parent allowing them to sign your name and handle financial affairs in your absence, unconscious state, or other circumstance. (Power-of-Attorney does not remain valid after death). The last document, a Trust, is started as a container for holding any assets that may be acquired before a more specific plan is made. This can be started with as little as $20.00 to begin the Corpus. Its existence will then provide a place to name for acquired stock, business interests, or other assets.

In the Appendices detailing the Generic Estate Plan, I provide a generic copy of each of these documents that you are free to copy and amend as necessary. This should only be used as stated for someone without a plan already in place and few assets under current consideration. Anyone who can afford to should get them done professionally. Also, please read the warning in other chapters regarding Power-of-Attorney before using.

Regarding my previous comments on not being a fan of regular Wills, most people believe that not having a Will causes them to get tied up in Probate Court settling Estate Issues. This may be true, but what they fail to consider is that a Will in and of itself initiates Probate. Wills are handled in Probate Court and cause court and attorney fees to be applied to an Estate. Having a traditional Will is like applying to the courts and hiring an attorney to watch over the transfer of your stuff—and boy, do they! Consider the fact that over 80% percent of Wills never end up following the plan laid out by the deceased. Pretty poor record, eh? An example: you own a hundred-acre farm that's been in the family for generations, and you want to hand it down to your three children and have them keep it in the family. The problem? Your Will initiates Probate and the children live out of town. So your attorney administers the Estate, pays bills, keeps the taxes current, and charges his fees—as does the Court and the Tax Man. So now, the property is worth $1.5 million and Court fees and attorney costs come to $300,000. The property has this value, but no cash is liquid. Your children have their own homes and mortgages, and none of them has $300,000 to pay the costs. Where does the money come from? You guessed it—the sale of the farm. Fees are paid and, yes, the children split the proceeds but no more family farm.

Real Estate has deeds and vehicles have Titles, etc. These ownership documents have your name on them and since you have died, the family has to take your Will to Probate Court and get permission for your name on all these Titles to be changed to another. That, in a nutshell, is the reason for Probate. If all this property were owned by artificial persons such as Corporations, LLC's, Trusts, etc., your death would not be equated with their death. In fact, artificial entities cannot die. When you die, the artificial entity still exists and whoever the next Beneficiary, Trustee, President, etc. is now controls the assets owned by that Entity. There is no need for asking Probate Courts to change titles or ownership of property, vehicle, financial accounts, etc.; the same owner still holds them, but a new person is in the driver's seat, so to speak.

Making a plan starts with setting goals and determining the reasons you want to accomplish them. There are many good books on setting goals and how to best achieve them. Among the usual suggestions they offer is writing them down, setting time frames, and starting with achievable mile markers. These same principles can be applied to your business plan. Are you starting a business because your primary goal is to work for yourself, or to work in a field you enjoy? Is it just a means of acquiring a larger home or a better car? Are you looking to replace the income of a particular job? Or are you looking to become a multi-millionaire? Do you have a service to provide or a product to sell? Are you building a business that you hope to sell to a larger firm at some point in the future? Or do you hope to have a company you can pass on to your children at some point?

There are no right or wrong answers to these questions, but the answers will be different for different individuals. Those differences may determine why you are leaning toward a Corporation while another prefers the Limited Partnership. Certain plans and business types lend themselves better to one entity type than another.

For instance, a group of attorneys that wants to share office expenses and caseload fluctuations might prefer to organize themselves as a Partnership, where they can share profits and at the same time have individual-hour billing to separately distinguish time and effort. This also has the advantage of each individual being responsible for their own taxes. Likewise, a person who opens a business to manufacture a product he invented and who will eventually leave the company to his children would not consider a Sole Proprietorship but might instead look at a C Corporation.

Will you have Partners who share the workload? Or Partners or Investors who will support you financially for a share of the business? Are you selling a product or providing a service to the public? Or to other businesses? Or both? Where will it physically be located? A state with or without an Income Tax? If you grow successful, would you still occupy only one location or more than one? Would you remain in one state or expand into others?

The answer to all these questions can have a bearing on the type of entity or even entities you should start. It may also help you to decide where the home office should be or in what state to Register or Incorporate. For instance, a business that may have branches in more than one state may want to consider Incorporation in a favorable non-income tax or business-friendly state such as Delaware, Nevada, or Wyoming. A business that is going to provide a product or service to the general public may want to consider having more than one company. One would be a front company that holds little or no assets to do business directly with the consumer, and the other in another jurisdiction that provides services or equipment to the front company. The latter would serve the purpose of holding and loaning or leasing the Capital Assets to the first company. This could make the second company the secured and first Creditor against the first company, holding a priority spot in front of complainants or suitors.

This arrangement can also be beneficial if your marketplace is in a high-tax jurisdiction. By having the front company do business in the high-tax state by receiving materials, loans, or leases from the second company in the non-tax state, you can govern where the profits show up and are considered to be earned. This enables the company located in the high-tax state to break even because of the price and payment of goods and services provided it by the company in the non-tax state. The end result is that your businesses will only have to pay a federal income tax rather than both a federal and state tax.

Now, before you accuse me of unfair dealing or worse, let me touch on a few issues regarding my aforementioned statements. First, my use of the term "front company" should not be equated with shell companies. You've probably read articles about such companies, the owners of which no one can determine, and that are often accused of cheating on taxes or defrauding the consumer. I am not at all referring to nor do I advocate such a thing. I am talking about businesses registered with the SOS's office, as legally mandated. Further, it is my opinion that if your business causes harm or damages to someone, you should be responsible and do what is right. However, should some consumer feel lucky that he has come up with an issue or has been damaged slightly yet now hopes to be placed on easy street for life by suing, you will be glad for the asset protection arrangement.

Regarding the so-called beating the high-tax state out of their tax, for simplicity of the concept I have described it in the context of someone having a front company and a second company. However, in actuality, these two companies would not have identical owners. Remember that persons at law can be both individuals and other type of entities. Therefore, a Trust is a person at law, and so is a Corporation. Bottom line? It needs to be done legally, not illegally, so get advice or profes-sional help if necessary. For those Socialists and Statists who believe no tax should be avoided and everyone should pay their fair share, I suggest reading a good book about the Federal Reserve and Fractional Reserve Banking. A short lesson in economics might also be helpful.

The main point is, only individuals pay taxes, either by

themselves or collectively. By taxing things collectively, such as Corporate Taxes, the amounts being paid directly by each individual is disguised or hidden. This allows the Collectivists to collect even more than the individual would typically put up with. Businesses are forced to incorporate the cost of taxes and regulations into the price of their goods and services, which are paid for by the end consumer. This means all taxes are paid by individual consumers because all taxes are paid by individuals. Therefore, if high-tax states succeed in closing every legal means of avoiding such taxes, they will succeed only in driving businesses out. This leaves fewer options, less competition, fewer jobs, and less wealth in that state. Sounds like a place I know, but enough of politics.

As you can see, defining what it is you are trying to accomplish and setting your goals is an essential step in deciding on the right business type and entity, as well as whether more than one is called for. Obviously, there are more questions and considerations than there are entity types to choose. So in some instances, it may simply come down to your preference. But those preferences should at least line up with your main concerns.

If your aim is to form a business, grow it, and then sell it to a bigger company, you wouldn't choose a Sole Proprietorship or even a Partnership. Most likely you would lean toward a Corporation, where the sale could be as simple as selling your stock. If you aim to create a company of which you will want to be and stay in control despite needing to sell more than 50% of it in order to raise or attract the Capital to realize your vision, you may choose to be the General Partner of a Limited Partnership.

The Sole Proprietorship, Corporation, LLC, and Limited Partnership all lend themselves well to a working President or visible leader who wants to be seen as the face of the company and the primary decision maker. But the fact is, the Trust or Corporation can be controlled more invisibly no matter who may appear to be in control. Many prideful people cannot bring themselves to forgo holding title or owning things personally. The advantages of that attitude may be many, as are the drawbacks. In the case of death or disability, Probate and long delays in asset transfer along with fees and taxes can be very costly. Catastrophic medical costs, fines, or a large judgment by a lawsuit against you will be satisfied against your personal and Business Assets. You are you until you die; you can't put yourself aside or change into another person. No matter how diversified you think your portfolio is—with stocks, bonds, Real Estate, or other investments—if it's is all in your name it's in the same basket as far as a judgment is concerned. However, an artificial entity—a legal person at law—can be easily dissolved, merged, or formed. Stocks and bonds and Real Estate and investments are really in separate baskets. A judgment against one is not a judgment against the other.

The person who realizes that they can't take it with them when they pass and who is less worried about the prestige of personal ownership may find he can use and enjoy all of the same assets without personal ownership. He may come to realize that managing and/or controlling his various baskets of assets is less costly, more anonymous, and every bit as satisfying. After all, you can't lose what you don't own and you're less likely to be a target in the first place. If you always have a nice car to drive, a cell phone to talk on, a roof over your head, etc., then why do you need to buy your own?

To own your stuff in your own name you have to go out and make a substantial income, pay taxes on it, and then have enough left over to pay for the stuff. A business, on the other hand, goes out and makes a large income, uses it to pay for all its stuff, and then pays taxes only on what's left over. Does that sound like the law favors business over individuals? You're right—it does! You may not consider that right or fair, but in the current economy, it is the reality. So you need to ask yourself if you are better off passing on personal property or control of property?

Just one short example, although there is an endless amount. John Doe has owned a commercial building in Anytown, USA, for the last 10 years. During that time, the transfer tax at the Registry of Deeds has gone up from .25% to .75% and new septic and sprinkler codes have been put in place. Inspections need to be passed at the time of any transfer in ownership. John Doe wants to sell the property, now valued at $2 million, but finds out these law changes will cost him $15,000 for the transfer tax, $25,000 for septic repairs, and $175,000 to install a sprinkler system—plus attorney fees and closing costs.

His sister Jane Doe-Smith bought a mirror-image commercial building at the same time as her brother and is also ready to dispose of it. Only when she bought hers, she placed it in JDS Enterprises, an artificial entity. Since the new regulations and transfer tax only apply at the time of sale of the Real Estate, she decides that rather than selling the $2 million property to a new owner, JDS Enterprises will continue to own the Real

Estate and she will sell her Beneficial Interest in it for $2.2 million. Her Beneficial Interest is private property and the sale of it has nothing to do with the commercial building, which continues to be owned by JDS Enterprises.

An additional problem to personally owned assets today is that if you should be a party to a failed marriage, your assets will most likely be considered marital assets subject to the courts and its decisions regarding the division of assets. No one should enter marriage in anticipation of its failure; however, in the structuring of businesses, there are more and less secure ways of doing things. One spouse running a well-managed company that is bringing income to herself and others should not have to be ruined because of an overly emotional or vindictive spouse. Many have been forced to sell businesses or assets that have become valuable because liquidity (available cash) did not allow for one spouse to buy out the value of the other's divorce award. In these cases, personally owning half the company versus being in control of a Trust or company that owns a company may make all the difference in the world. Again, for the sensitive, I am not advocating for one spouse over another or for depriving anyone of something they are entitled to. I am saying there are ways of securing agreements that will stand a better chance of having financial interests remain as they were planned for in the event one party becomes disagreeable or destructive at a future time. Splitting the income derived from an income-producing asset may be preferable to forgoing the asset altogether.

Proper planning is important. With this in mind, I will now review the advantages and disadvantages of the various entity types and offer some creative suggestions, such as Bearer

Shares, Stockholder Trusts, making your Home Trust a partner to raise capital, etc. But do not get overly bogged down with being an expert before you get started. Trust your increased understanding. If you have a current business or an opportunity to start one, do it. The nice thing about businesses and agreements is you can always make changes and improvements as you go. If you start a Corporation, for instance, and hold the stock yourself, you can always create a Trust to hold it later after your Corporation begins to get successful. You can always start a business to do business with your existing business, or you can sell it or go into Partnership with another person at any time. So don't spend too much time worrying about getting it 100% perfect to begin with or you may never start.

For those with unusual or unique situations, remember that contracts are agreements between two or more persons and that persons at law are not only you and me but include artificial entities. This knowledge may allow you to get the creative juices flowing. For example, even though a General Partner has full liability for the debts and actions of the Partnership, a Corporation may fill the position of General Partner. So although the Corporation has full liability as a General Partner, the individuals involved in the Corporation still have their Limited Liability because they are Corporate Officers. Corporations can also be Trustees of Trusts. Trusts can hold the stock and be the owner of a Corporation rather than an individual(s).

Although on public record Corporate Officers hold positions such as President, Secretary, and Treasurer, hired employees who do not own even one share of stock in the company may hold these positions. The creative interactions among business entities, their managers, and actual Beneficial Owners may be as varied as the imagination.

The key to choosing the right entity or entities for your purposes is to outline your goals and purposes. Even if some of the items on your list appear to be at odds with each other, there is a way to achieve your objectives with a "can do" attitude! In conjunction with the type of entity and ownership structure, do not forget to review the example situations and discussion about jurisdiction in Chapter 2.

Most likely, the opportunity you are considering or the business you want to start or have already begun has arisen near where you live. The type of service, product, or industry you are involved in may dictate when and with whom you do business. Many sales and service companies can easily choose the best jurisdiction to be the base for their company, and a "non-income tax" state like Delaware, Nevada, or Wyoming can be a no-brainer. Other business types like manufacturing, and businesses with large physical inventories and local assets or special licenses, may have a more difficult time basing themselves outside the jurisdiction of their marketplace. Although any business may register in these business-favorable states, some may also be forced to register as a Foreign Corporation within the state in which they are physically doing business. In some of those instances, it may be simpler to register domestically and get creative about the Ownership Interest Holder and what type of entity that could be. Or create a second entity in a favorable state in which to do some business, thereby creating a valve for adjusting where profits materialize.

CHAPTER 15

Profit & Loss, Balance Sheet, and Cash Flow

Today's computers and their associated programs for business functions save both business owners and their accountants untold hours of work and analysis. Accounting software packages such as QuickBooks, Peachtree (now Sage 50cloud), and several others can separate and categorize financial transactions into multiple time frames and data views at the click of a mouse. Transactions entered just once into the program can be displayed and printed into numerous ledgers and reports. These can help you to determine the company's financial health and position as well as ready tax information for filing.

Having a basic understanding of a few of the main reports looked at by accountants, bankers, and investors can help you anticipate what information they will focus on. Whether you are looking for loans or investors or anticipating tax consequences, understanding what these reports reveal will be beneficial.

Every business owner needs to have a handle on his Profit & Loss Statement, Balance Sheet, and Cash Flow. A Profit & Loss Statement is a report that lists Income Items and compares them against Expense Items to show if you are gaining or losing over specific periods of time. Although these reports can be made to show the activity from periods as short as one day to as long as the business has existed, typically analysis would be done in monthly, quarterly, or annual reports. In Figures 8 and 9 to follow, you will see a Profit & Loss Statement for "Acme Company, Inc." showing a one-year report from January 1st through December 31st of a given year. The letters in red, which will be referred to as "Tags," indicate the individual items that will be discussed.

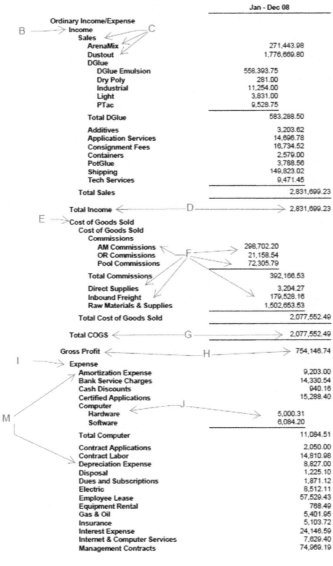

A → **Acme Company, Inc.**
Profit & Loss
January through December 2008

	Jan - Dec 08
Ordinary Income/Expense	
B → Income C	
Sales	
ArenaMix	271,443.98
Dustout	1,776,669.80
DGlue	
DGlue Emulsion	558,393.75
Dry Poly	281.00
Industrial	11,254.00
Light	3,831.00
PTac	9,528.75
Total DGlue	583,288.50
Additives	3,203.62
Application Services	14,696.78
Consignment Fees	16,734.52
Containers	2,579.00
PotGlue	3,788.56
Shipping	149,823.02
Tech Services	9,471.45
Total Sales	2,831,699.23
Total Income ← D →	2,831,699.23
E → Cost of Goods Sold	
Cost of Goods Sold	
Commissions	
AM Commissions	298,702.20
OR Commissions F	21,158.54
Pool Commissions	72,305.79
Total Commissions	392,166.53
Direct Supplies	3,204.27
Inbound Freight	179,528.16
Raw Materials & Supplies	1,502,653.53
Total Cost of Goods Sold	2,077,552.49
Total COGS ← G →	2,077,552.49
Gross Profit ← H →	754,146.74
I → Expense	
Amortization Expense	9,203.00
Bank Service Charges	14,330.54
Cash Discounts	940.16
Certified Applications	15,288.40
Computer	
Hardware ← J →	5,000.31
M Software	6,084.20
Total Computer	11,084.51
Contract Applications	2,050.00
Contract Labor	14,810.98
Depreciation Expense	8,827.00
Disposal	1,225.10
Dues and Subscriptions	1,871.12
Electric	8,512.11
Employee Lease	57,529.43
Equipment Rental	768.49
Gas & Oil	5,401.95
Insurance	5,103.72
Interest Expense	24,146.59
Internet & Computer Services	7,629.40
Management Contracts	74,969.19

Page 1

Figure 8

Acme Company, Inc.
Profit & Loss
January through December 2008

	Jan - Dec 08
Marketing	
Advertising	3,080.23
Internet Promotions	6,967.14
Promotional Discounts	52,404.14
Total Marketing	62,451.51
Postage	2,971.41
Professional Fees	
Accounting	10,883.75
Legal Fees	3,264.49
Total Professional Fees	14,148.24
Rent	
AZ Warehouse	40,990.37
MA Headquarters	54,000.00
Panama Warehouse	1,934.50
Total Rent	96,924.87
Repairs	
Building Repairs	1,139.01
Computer Repairs	134.99
Equipment Repairs	3,079.00
Total Repairs	4,353.00
Shipping Costs	153,764.56
Snow Removal	2,100.00
Supplies	
Marketing	878.27
Office	7,113.17
Warehouse	
AZ Warehouse	6,964.36
MA Warehouse	13,485.96
Panama Warehouse	597.30
Total Warehouse	21,047.62
Total Supplies	29,039.06
Taxes	
Taxes - Other	1,136.77
Total Taxes	1,136.77
Telephone	13,136.09
Tolls & Parking	127.90
Trademark & Research Royalties	9,267.00
Travel & Ent	
Meals	1,569.58
Travel	35,005.78
Total Travel & Ent	36,575.36
Warranty	357.50
Total Expense ←————K————→	690,044.96
Net Ordinary Income	64,101.78
Other Income/Expense	
Other Income	
Interest Income	256.10
Total Other Income	256.10
Net Other Income	256.10
Net Income ←————L————→	64,357.88

Figure 9

In Figure 8, you will note that Tag A points to the company name, the report type (Profit & Loss), and the time period (in this case, Jan 1 – Dec 31 08). Running this report any time after January 1st of the new year would give a complete view of the Income and Expenses of the previous year.

Tag B shows the category "Income." Tag C notes the "Income" category further divided into sub-categories—first of "Sales" and then of the various "Sales Items or "Product Names." The list of "Income Items" and their sub-categories are totaled at Tag D. It should be noted here that the business owners could have simply had a single category line for "Income" itself. Or they might have the category of "Income" with sub-categories of "Sales" and "Service" but choose not to individualize sub-categories for the individual product names; likewise for all the "Expense" and other categories that are sub-categorized. The business owner, in conjunction with his accountant and/or bookkeeper, will need to determine the extent of time and effort he wants to be documented. Less sub-categorization means less ability to create detailed reports and analysis in the future; more means many more options for obtaining detail quickly about a variety of issues.

For instance, should a manufacturer of several products suddenly discover its inability to obtain a certain raw material or part for one of its products, a detailed total of sales for the products affected would help in computing the effect it would have on total sales. However, this may be impossible to determine if all sales are simply lumped into a single category of "Product Sales." Or, at the least, it may make the analysis of the question much more difficult and time-consuming than further sub-categorization would have in the first place.

On our Profit & Loss Statement, at Tag E you will see the category "Cost of Goods Sold." "Cost of Goods Sold" or "Cost of Sales" are categories often seen on the Profit & Loss Statement of manufacturers and product sales companies. In our sample, you will see that Tag F shows that this category has also been sub-categorized. Although some bookkeepers may show these same costs within the list of "Expense" categories, certain costs that have a directly proportional relationship to each sale or good are better classified this way.

Certain Expenses like Rent, Electricity, and Insurance, for instance, are considered the "Indirect Costs" of any particular product sold or produced. Therefore, they are properly listed under "Expenses." Although you may not be able to do without them in the business, they are still indirect and occur whether or not you sell a single item. "Expenses" are part of what needs to be controlled and overcome in order to have a profitable business.

"Cost of Goods," on the other hand, only occurs based on the sales or production of another product or sale. For example, let's say you make and sell Widgets. The Widgets are created from a block of material for which you pay $3 for every Widget made. You also pay $1 as a sales commission for each one sold. If you sell your Widgets for $7 each, your direct costs or "Cost of Goods" is $4—the $3 material cost plus the $1 commission on each. These are direct costs because if sales slow down and you refrain from producing more Widgets until they begin to sell again, you also will not have additional material and commission costs at that time.

Take note of Tag H on our Profit & Loss Statement—the company's "Gross Profit." Notice that this amount was arrived at by subtracting "Cost of Goods" (Tag G) from "Total Income" (Tag D). In the previous example of Widgets, this would be taking the sales price of $7 and subtracting the "Cost of Goods" (Widget material and commission) of $4 to arrive at our "Gross Profit" on this Widget of $3. This does not mean the company's "Profit" will be $3. From this "Gross Profit," all the other Expenses of running the company need to be paid. If you can control and minimize the Expenses to the point that the Gross Profit—or, in our example, the $3 from each Widget—is not totally used up you will have a company Profit; otherwise, you will have a Loss.

As you can see, the use of the category "Cost of Goods" or "Cost of Sales" gives a more accurate read and picture of the company's position. In both our Profit & Loss Statement and our Widget example, saying that the company's Total Income (Tag D) should be seen as its Gross Profit (Tag H) would be to inflate the amount available to cover "Expenses." This would be true in the same way it would be inaccurate to say we make $7 per Widget on each sale when each and every Widget costs us a constant $4. Therefore, it is much more accurate to show $3 per Widget after "Direct Expenses" to see what I have to overcome the cost of Rent, Electric, and other expenses. See more on this idea under "Cost Analysis."

Now let us move to Tag I, the "Expenses" on our Profit & Loss Statement. Just as in the upper section under "Income," you will notice that "Expenses" are also sub-categorized into various individual types such as Electric, Insurance, Rent, etc., and that some of these are further sub-categorized, such as "Computers" at Tag J into "Hardware" and "Software." Again, the more detail, the easier future decision making will be when you are looking to make changes that could affect the bottom line.

In Figure 9, Tag K ("Total Expenses") displays the total amount of "Expenses." This amount, subtracted from Tag H ("Gross Profit") in Figure 8, results in "Net Income" at Tag L in Figure 9. "Net Income" is the last line on the Profit & Loss Statement, hence the term "the Bottom Line."

In Figure 8, two "Expense" items shown on our Profit & Loss Statement as Tag M are "Amortization Expense" and "Depreciation Expense." Each of these line items is derived using accounting formulas and schedules for the allowable recapture of Capital and the estimated useful life of "Fixed Assets." The annual amount of allowable deductions shown on the Profit & Loss Statement for said period is a portion of the total "Accumulated Amortization" and "Depreciation" shown on the Balance Sheet to follow (see Figure 10, Tag J).

Amortization is the rate of recapture of Capital, or the rate at which you are allowed to deduct as "Expenses" those funds initially spent to start the business, do research or product development, or the cost of intellectual or other intangible "Expenses."

Depreciation is the rate at which a company is allowed to deduct as "Expenses" certain Capital Expenditures, such as the purchase of industrial machinery, vehicles, or other equipment that will have a useful life beyond one year. In other words, if your business requires a truck as part of its equipment and you go out this year and pay $20,000 for a truck for that business, you will not be allowed to deduct the entire $20,000 from the business income for that year.

Instead, you will see from a schedule approved by the IRS

that they allow you to deduct, or expense, only $4,000 that first year and another $4,000 each year for five years until the $20,000 original cost can be completely Expensed or Depreciated. This is partially due to the assumption that the truck will be a useful piece of equipment for five years. So when you buy the truck, the value of $20,000 is added to the Balance Sheet of your business. At year-end, when you take the $4,000 Allowable Expense Deduction, you can reduce your Income on the Profit & Loss Statement with the Depreciation Expense.

At the same time, you mark a negative $4,000 value as Accumulated Depreciation (see Figure 10, Tag J) on the company's Balance Sheet, which lowers the value of the truck to $16,000. This process is repeated annually for all such Assets until they have no appreciable value. You may continue to use the truck beyond the five years to make money in your business if it still functions, but it will have no further value on the Balance Sheet nor deductions on the Profit & Loss Statement.

These deductions for money spent years ago are sometimes called phantom deductions because in the current year, when new assets are not being paid for, you get to write off expenses from your Net Income that did not actually occur that year.

So the Profit & Loss Statement is a snapshot in time showing the business owner's "Income" versus "Expenses," while the Balance Sheet is a picture of "Assets" versus "Liabilities" at any point in time from the start of the business to the current date. The most basic equation in Accounting is: Assets = Liabilities + Owners Equity. The Balance Sheet shows the relationship of those three items to each other at all times. As a person's blood pressure and temperature are to health, the Balance Sheet is to the health of your Business.

Think of a Balanced Scale, and that is how to view the relationship between "Assets" on one side and "Liabilities & Equity" on the other.

Balance Sheet

It has to balance

Everything a company has—from checking and savings account, investments, Real Estate, furniture and equipment, and vehicles to tools, raw materials, product inventory, and receivables (money owed it)—are Assets of the company. All these items make up the "Assets" side of the Balance Sheet.

Everything a company owes—from credit card bills, leases, and loans on property and equipment to vehicles, tools and accounts payable for raw materials, electricity, or any other outstanding bills—are its Liabilities. All these Liabilities are listed on the Liabilities side of the Balance Sheet.

Equity or Owners' Equity is the amount of value remaining after subtracting all the Liabilities from the value of the Assets. This amount is a positive number if it reflects what is due the owners, and a negative amount if it represents what the owners would need to add to the company to make it solvent. Although equity is not a debt or a Liability, it goes on the Liability side of the scale because, from the viewpoint of the company, all Assets belong to somebody. They are either owed to a Creditor or an owner. Therefore, Assets always need to equal Liabilities plus Owners' Equity (Assets = Liabilities + Owners' Equity).

In the following Balance Sheet for "Acme Company, Inc." (Figures 10 and 11), again look for the letters in red to indicate the items that will be discussed.

Acme Company, Inc.
A ────➤ **Balance Sheet**
As of December 31, 2008

	Dec 31, 08
B ➤ **ASSETS**	
Current Assets	
Checking/Savings	
Connoco Escrow	1,352.91
Lowell Checking	17,116.09
Savings Account	2,576.87
Sovereign Checking	88,699.51
Total Checking/Savings	109,745.38
Accounts Receivable	
Accounts Receivable	319,768.48
Total Accounts Receivable	319,768.48
Other Current Assets	
Loans Receivable	
Advance Commissions	-223.49
Total Loans Receivable	-223.49
Inventory Asset	108,597.92
Prepaid Expense	8,819.77
Total Other Current Assets	117,194.20
Total Current Assets	546,708.06
Fixed Assets	
Equipment	
Air Compressor	2,097.18
Dock Plate	1,261.53
Fork Truck	42,288.00
Ind Floor Scale	1,500.00
Pallet Jack	1,030.10
Pressure Washer	303.27
Viscometer	1,098.00
Yard Ramp	10,315.00
Acc/Depr Equipment	
Acc/Depr	-22,247.00
Total Acc/Depr Equipment	-22,247.00
Total Equipment	37,646.08
Total Fixed Assets	37,646.08
Other Assets	
DGE SA Stock	4,658.00
Research & Development	
Research & Development	100,400.00
A/A Research & Development	-100,400.00
Total Research & Development	0.00
Security Deposit	
APS - Electric Co AZ	1,495.00
AZ Warehouse	3,786.00
MA Warehouse	9,000.00
NewWay Lease	4,000.00
Total Security Deposit	18,281.00
Total Other Assets	22,939.00
TOTAL ASSETS	607,293.14

Figure 10

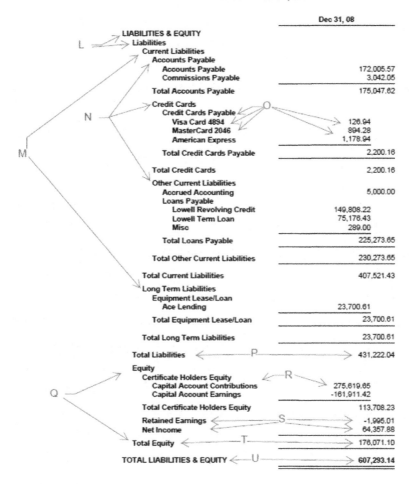

Figure 11

In Figure 10, Tag A displays the company name, report type (Balance Sheet), and date of the report. The top half begins with the main category, Tag B, which refers to "Assets." This category is sub-categorized into "Current Assets," "Fixed Assets," and "Other Assets," as shown by Tag C. Each of these, in turn, is sub-categorized to better describe the Assets that are being valued. For example, "Current Assets," shown by Tag D, is sub-categorized into "Checking/Savings," "Accounts Receivable," and "Other Current Assets." "Checking/Savings" is divided into the various named bank accounts shown by Tag E. Each line item is totaled and sub-totaled with its group, for a total of the main sub-category, such as "Total Current Assets" at Tag F. Whether broken down into layers of detail, like under "Fixed Assets" with its various locations and pieces of equipment at Tag G, or divided into just broad categories, these will all be totaled at some point as "Total Assets" at Tag K.

Before moving to the bottom half of the Balance Sheet, take a look at Tag J, which is the total of "Equipment" under "Fixed Assets." Then look at Tag I and note the negative entry, which reflects the amount of allowable deductions or depreciated value of the "Fixed Assets" listed. The original amounts across from each equipment piece under "Fixed Assets" (Tag H) indicate the original value or amount paid for the item. These original amounts reduced by the "Accumulated Depreciation" amount is what brings you the current "Total Equipment" amount shown at Tag J. The portion of the amount of "Acc/Depr." (Tag I) allowed for that year is the amount transferred and found on our Profit & Loss Statement (Figure 8, Tag M), as previously discussed.

The second half of our Balance Sheet, Figure 11, begins like the top half, with its main category "Liabilities & Equity" at Tag L. This category also has been divided into sub-categories of "Current Liabilities" and "Long Term Liabilities" at Tag M.

Each of these is divided into its own sub-categories as shown by Tag N, as has each of those—for example, "Credit Cards" at Tag O showing the individual named accounts and balances. As with the Asset side of the report, all categories culminate in "Total Liabilities" at Tag P. Added to this amount at the bottom of the report is the section displaying the "Equity" in the company. Usually, this section (Tag Q) will display categories such as "Common Stock," "Partners Equity," "Original Capital," "Additional Paid-In Capital," or a combination of these (see Tag R). Added to this category will be one called "Retained Earnings" and one for "Net Income" (see Tag S). These all add up to Tag T, "Total Equity."

"Original Capital," "Common Stock," or "Partner Contributions" are fairly straightforward; these are the amounts originally used to start the business or Capitalize it. "Retained Earnings" is the figure showing "Net Income" amounts from prior years that the company continues to hold and hasn't yet distributed to the owners or stockholders. In the early years of a business, this figure may be negative, as Capital or loans provide for its start-up while profits are only anticipated. The "Net Income" figure reflects the Income for the current year and at times, especially in the first years, may also be negative.

These amounts in the Equity section are totaled by adding "Initial" and "Added Capital" to "Retained Earnings" and "Net Income," less any distributions resulting in "Total Equity" (Tag T). This amount is added to "Total Liabilities" (Tag P), to arrive at "Total Liabilities & Equity"—the last line of the Balance Sheet, Tag U. You will notice this amount is equal to "Total Assets" (Tag K), showing that the Balance Sheet is balanced because Assets = Liabilities + Equity. On our Profit & Loss

Statement (Figure 9), you will also note that the amount of "Net Income" (Tag S) on the Balance Sheet is equal to and was derived from the Bottom Line (Tag L).

Before we leave the Balance Sheet, I would like to point out that one of the items under "Other Current Assets" (Figure 10, Tag D) is a category for "Inventory Assets" (see Tag V). Not all companies have inventories, but indeed many do. Some companies have small, just-in-time sales inventories; some have huge storehouses. Some have one or a few items; others, hundreds of different items. Depending on your type of business, the kind and amount of inventory needing management will determine what kind of system is required by your company. Again, this is a topic for a whole other book, so my purpose here is to simply let you know that such things may need to be taken into consideration and further researched. Perishable goods, for instance, need to be rotated to ensure that items received first are sold before newer deliveries. Systems of quality control often need to be instituted. Labeling and number systems that provide specific information are important for tracking the vendor that provided them or to be able to isolate and locate other such deliveries. Pricing and taxing issues come into play with multiple deliveries of items of varying costs.

If I pay $1 for a Widget this month and $2 three months from now, when a Widget is finally sold what was my cost? The average of all bought? Or do I sell the one I bought for $1 first? On another note, do I use a system of average or actual cost? Or a system of "first in first out," "first in last out," or "last in first out"? Hopefully, I have made my point. You should keep a list of the important factors to consider for your particular business; the better thought out, the better and more appropriate your system will be.

The "Cash Flow Report" is another important barometer for the business owner to be familiar with. This report displays the various financial accounts and their available balances at a given point in time. It compares these balances and their increases and decreases over the period of time displayed, showing whether available cash is increasing or decreasing. This knowledge is crucial to reconciling your Receivables (money owed to you) with your Payables (money you owe). Knowing how much is in the checking account now and being able to forecast when and how much your customers will be paying in the near future allows you to see if the bills you owe and the commitments you make can be covered by available cash. Even companies with vast amounts of Fixed Assets, Real Estate, and Current Orders for business can get in a bind and hurt their reputation and credit if they lose sight of short-term cash flow and current obligations.

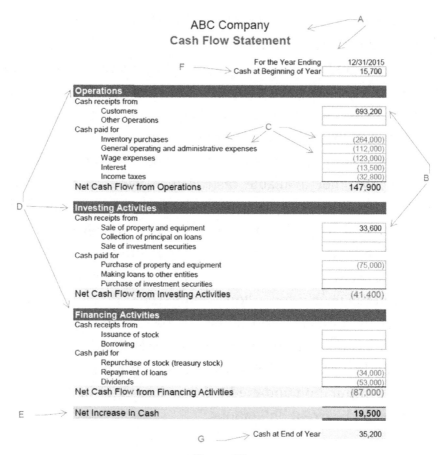

Figure 12

In Figure 12, "Cash Flow Statement" for the "ABC Company," you will note that Tag A displays the company name, report type, date of the report, and time frame, as in the previous reports. "Statements of Cash Flows" present the inflows in positive figures while the outflows are shown in negative figures, sometimes with a minus sign or in parentheses indicating the same. Tag B points to inflows while Tag C show some outflows. Cash inflows and outflows are usually classified into three activities—"Operations," "Investment Activities," and "Financial Activities," as shown at Tag D.

"Operating Activities" refer to the main operations of the company, such as the provision of professional services, acquisition of inventories, supplies, collection of accounts, payment of accounts, etc. "Investment Activities" involve where the company places money long term, while "Financial Activities" refer to where the company gets its funds, such as investments, owners, or bank financing.

After cash inflows and outflows are summed up, the net increase or decrease in cash is computed (see Tag E, "Net Increase in Cash"). This figure added to Cash at the beginning of the period under consideration—in this case, Beginning of Year (Tag F)—will give you the new cash position at the end of the period—in this case, year-end (Tag G). Having a net increase in cash at the end of any period of time as opposed to a decrease is certainly the target of the business owner. Decreasing Cash Flow may indicate that the company's liquid assets are decreasing.

As can be seen from this short overview of Profit & Loss Statements, Balance Sheets, and Cash Flow Reports, orderly and timely entry of data and a working knowledge of what they display can be crucial in keeping a handle on your business. It will help you see troubling trends and make changes to correct them earlier rather than later. It will also present you as a knowledgeable business owner to vendors, bankers, and investors should you ever require their aid or collaboration. Always remember money follows management. Good management!

CHAPTER 16

Budgets and Cost Analysis

Budgeting is another financial tool used to help keep spending in line with your goals and available income. A personal home budget usually consists of adding all the standard bills—rent, electric, heat, groceries, vehicles, etc.—into weekly or monthly amounts and subtracting the final amount from the amount of income received weekly, biweekly, or monthly. The budget determines your discretionary income, if any. With a business, this may be slightly more involved, but the principle is the same.

A new business venture should be started in conjunction with a "Fixed Cost Analysis," which we shall only touch on lightly. For an ongoing business, budgeting can take various forms depending on type, size, and number of departments. In the beginning, while Capital is being relied on above projected income, starting with cost estimates and priorities, certain amounts should be allocated to each category. In an existing business, one method would be to take the previous actual costs and allow certain percentage increases or decreases for each account category, allowing for inflation of supply costs, and changes in goals to determine such increases or decreases. In an effort to expand the Bottom Line, expenses in each category or company department may be targeted for percent decreases across the board.

As mentioned, before starting a new business a Fixed Cost Analysis should be done to help find the budget starting point as well as determine the viability of the business idea itself. Some claim that 80% to 90% of businesses fail in their first year. I am not sure how accurate this estimate is, but certainly, a large number of companies do fail in their early stages. In my experience, this occurs most often because of a lack of realistic planning, not having a specific target market, and being under-capitalized. Insufficient Capital is by far the leading cause, although this is also related to poor planning. In other words, not having recognized the amount of capital needed in the beginning. There are many stories of people starting a business with only a few cents in their pocket and becoming unbelievably wealthy. There are probably far more stories about people starting a business, losing everything, and then going and getting a job. We just don't hear about them because they don't make for very inspirational reading.

If you have an excellent product or service, you may end up being successful without Capital to start, but you will have a far greater chance of success if you plan properly and set aside the necessary funds called for by the plan.

After determining the product or service you plan to provide, you need to investigate and decide if there is a need and/or desire for such a product or service. Then you have to establish how large a marketplace there is for it. Is someone else serving this same market? And can you compete and get some of it? If all that is positive, then you need to figure out what it is going to cost to bring it to market. The Fixed Cost Analysis is a good starting point.

Let's say I want to start my own company, and I have recently invented a "doohickey" I think everyone will want once they see it. I decide to call it a "Widget" and plan on starting a business to produce and sell it called "Widget Co." I plan on using commission-only salespeople. I will need a building to assemble the product and ship it out and a receptionist who is available during weekly business hours. I will also need to hire an assembler to put the Widgets together. The materials to make each Widget will cost me $15, and I plan on paying a $4 Sales Commission for each one sold. It will also cost $2 each to package the Widget. This adds up to $21 cost per unit. I plan to sell it for $49.95. So $49.95 minus $21 in costs will leave me a margin of $28.95 for each one sold.

After finding a place to rent and getting estimates of the various costs and expenses I will have, I put together my analysis.

	A	C	D	E	F	G	H	I
1	**Widget Co.**	**Cost**	**Analysis**					
2					7 Day	5 Day	Hrly 7 Days	Hrly 5 Day
3	Totals :	$85,360.00	$7,113.33	$1,641.54	$233.86	328.31	29.23	41.04
4	Items :	Yrly.	Mnthly.	Wkly.	Day	Wrk Day	Hrly 7 Days	Hrly 5 Day
5	Rent	$12,000.00	$1,000.00	$230.77	$32.88	$46.15	$4.11	$5.77
6	Electric	$1,800.00	$150.00	$34.62	$4.93	$6.92	$0.62	$0.87
7	Telephone	$2,400.00	$200.00	$46.15	$6.58	$9.23	$0.82	$1.15
8	Receptionist ($10 per hr.)	$27,664.00	$2,305.33	$532.00	$75.79	$106.40	$9.47	$13.30
9	Assembler ($15 per hr.)	$41,496.00	$3,458.00	$798.00	$113.69	$159.60	$14.21	$19.95
10		$0.00	$0.00	$0.00	$0.00	$0.00	$0.00	$0.00
11		$0.00	$0.00	$0.00	$0.00	$0.00	$0.00	$0.00
12		$0.00	$0.00	$0.00	$0.00	$0.00	$0.00	$0.00
13		$0.00	$0.00	$0.00	$0.00	$0.00	$0.00	$0.00
14		$0.00	$0.00	$0.00	$0.00	$0.00	$0.00	$0.00
15								
16								
17								
18	Totals :	$85,360.00	$7,113.33	$1,641.54	$233.86	$328.31	$29.23	$41.04
19	Time Period	Yrly.	Mnthly.	Wkly.	Day	Wrk Day	Hrly 7 Days	Hrly 5 Day
20	# of Widgets Needed							
21	to cover overhead costs:	2950	247	58	9	12	2	2
22	($ needed / Profit Margin)							
23	$28.95							

Figure 13

Figure 13 provides a snapshot of the "Widget Co. Cost

Analysis" spreadsheet used to analyze the estimated costs. Listed in column A, in rows 5 to 9, you will see the various Fixed Expenses. I have listed Rent, Electric, Telephone, a receptionist at $10 per hour, and an assembler at $15 per hour; these are all costs that are independent of selling a single Widget.

These are the costs of opening a place of business ready to make and sell my product, whether I sell none per day or many. In fact, since my income from this business will come from making and selling Widgets, I need to determine the fixed costs so I can compute just how many of them will have to be sold to realize a profit.

Therefore, across from each Item listed in column A, you will see in column C what I have estimated the Annual costs of each to be (see column C, rows 5 to 9). Continuing across the column, you will see how each item row further breaks down the Yearly estimate into Monthly, Daily, Weekly, and Hourly amounts. There are two Daily Columns, one column labeled "Day," representing a five-day week, and one labeled "Wrk Day," based on dividing Weekly Costs into Daily Costs assuming seven days a week for the Day column and five days a week for the Wrk Day column. Additionally, I have likewise split the Daily Costs into Hourly Costs. Each Hourly column is also based, respectively, on the five- or seven-day week. The combined total of the amounts in each column is displayed in row 3 following across from the label "Totals" at column A3.

Column C, row 3 shows an Annual "Fixed Overhead" of $85,360 divided into its hourly breakdown (based on eight hours, seven days a week), which is $29.23. In my initial cost target, this hourly amount of $29.23 will cover the costs of a business open eight hours a day, seven days a week, with two full-time employees. My income from product sales needs to cover this overhead before I can have a profitable business. If I will operate the business only five days a week the cost needed per hour to overcome Fixed Overhead becomes $41.04 per hour.

Figure 14 provides a picture of the Cost of Goods amount mentioned. It shows that each unit (Widget) requires $15 for material, a $4 commission, and $2 to package. Assuming a $49.95 price of sale, less these Cost of Goods ($21), the company will clear $28.95 each. So if $41.04 is the cost per hour of business overhead (based on a five-day work week), I will need to sell more than one Widget per hour.

	A	B
1	**COG = Cost of Goods:**	
3	Material Cost per unit	$15.00
4	Sales Commission per unit	$4.00
5	Packaging	$2.00
7	Cost Per Unit	$21.00
8		
9	Sales Price Per Unit	$49.95
10	Subtract Cost of Goods	($21.00)
12	Profit Margin Per Unit:	$28.95
13		
14		
15		
16	Note: Production Time!	
17	(additional shifts / profits)	
18	If 2 units an hour can be made:	
19	Then: 2 X Profit Margin Per Unit ($28.95 ea.)	$57.90
20	Subtract cost of overhead per hour (5 day)	$41.04
22	Gross Profit per hour (pre other expenses):	$16.86
23		
24	**Annually on 5 day work week = $35,068.80**	

Figure 14

Looking at Figure 14, column A, row 17 you will see that with one assembler to build the Widgets, we have estimated that two units can be made per hour. So if I can also sell these two units per hour, or 80 units per week, then my forecast is positive. Two units each hour will supply the business with a margin of $28.95 each, so that amount multiplied by two will yield a margin of $57.90. Subtract from this the hourly cost of being in business, $41.04, and the business will be left with $16.86 above costs each hour. This would compute to a business profit in this case of $35,068.80 per year based on this Analysis.

This Analysis certainly is a simple one; payroll taxes and employee sick time are left out for simplicity. Assumptions are made as to the Sales Price being realistic and the idea that two or more units per hour can be sold. Looking at the columns for the Daily, Weekly, Monthly, and Annual amounts used to calculate the overhead, we see that it is necessary to sell 247 units per month, or 2,950 units per year, for this model to work (see Figure 13, columns C and D, row 21). After arriving at these realities, I need to determine whether a marketplace that can absorb this quantity of Widgets actually exists and I can get a big enough share of it.

If I conclude that my assumptions are indeed realistic and the target market is far larger than the minimum size I need to survive in business, then I can look at going beyond the minimums. At this point, I may rethink the numbers. I would determine how many Widgets per week or month a salesperson might need to sell to make a living wage. I might run the numbers to see about adding one or more assemblers and expanding to three shifts. Although this would increase the total overhead needed for the same period, it might decrease the cost per unit. I would not need a receptionist for the second and third shifts, and one month's rent would be the same whether I use the building eight or 24 hours a day. When Fixed Overhead becomes steady and is covered by a certain number of unit sales, all sales above this point become more and more profitable. In other words, the more Widgets sold, the less per unit required to go toward a relatively fixed and steady overhead.

	A	C	D	E	F	G	H	I
1	**Widget Co.**	**Cost**	**Analysis**					
2					7 Day	5 Day	Hrly 7 Days	Hrly 5 Day
3	Totals :	$296,140.00	$24,678.33	$5,695.00	$811.34	1,139.00	101.42	142.38
4	Items :	Yrly.	Mnthly.	Wkly.	Day	Wrk Day	Hrly 7 Days	Hrly 5 Day
5	Rent	$12,000.00	$1,000.00	$230.77	$32.88	$46.15	$4.11	$5.77
6	Electric	$1,800.00	$150.00	$34.62	$4.93	$6.92	$0.62	$0.87
7	Telephone	$2,400.00	$200.00	$46.15	$6.58	$9.23	$0.82	$1.15
8	Receptionist ($10 per hr.)	$27,664.00	$2,305.33	$532.00	$75.79	$106.40	$9.47	$13.30
9	2 Assemblers ($15 per hr	$82,992.00	$6,916.00	$1,596.00	$227.38	$319.20	$28.42	$39.90
10	2 Assemblers (2nd Shift)	$82,992.00	$6,916.00	$1,596.00	$227.38	$319.20	$28.42	$39.90
11	2 Assemblers (3rd Shift)	$82,992.00	$6,916.00	$1,596.00	$227.38	$319.20	$28.42	$39.90
12	Additional Electricity	$1,500.00	$125.00	$28.85	$4.11	$5.77	$0.51	$0.72
13	Additional Phone	$800.00	$66.67	$15.38	$2.19	$3.08	$0.27	$0.38
14	Additional Misc	$1,000.00	$83.33	$19.23	$2.74	$3.85	$0.34	$0.48

Figure 15

Figure 15 shows the increased costs of adding two assemblers for each of three shifts. Although the cost per hour based on eight hours a day rises if you divide the $142.38 an hour by the added costs over 24 hours of operations, your needs fall to $47.46 per hour. This is not much higher than the $41.04 previously required. But now, rather than producing 16 units a day you, are producing 96 units. This will produce an annual Gross Profit after the Cost of Goods of $426,441 as opposed to only $35,068 annually. Once you perform your Analysis and become confident about your ability to meet the minimums and excited about the potentials, then you just might have a viable business venture.

Now, how much are you and/or someone else willing to bet on the accuracy and reality of your Analysis? Some time and effort? Some money? Both? Will you quit your full-time job? Start the business in your spare time? Use your savings to secure the building lease, tools, and employee salary? What if sales start slower than expected? How long can you finance the difference? Are you confident enough to borrow against your home or ask someone to invest or become a Partner? These are all serious questions. Going into business always involves some risk. Answering these questions realistically and starting prudently in regard to the amount of Capital needed offers you the best chance of success. Anything less jeopardizes the time, effort, and money you do put in.

Previously, after touching on the subject of inventory, I mentioned how there are many nuances involved and that further research may be needed depending on your business type. This same caveat can be applied to product sales. As with inventory, I mention product sales only to point out the need for further research into the many subtle distinctions and considerations necessary for developing a product sales plan for certain business types.

There are many such considerations. For example, questions such as, do I advertise only and sell with on-site owner presence? Do I hire salespeople and start my own sales department? Do I pay them base pay plus commission? Or commission only? Do I hire an outside agency to carry my product along with others? Do I protect and offer territories? Or do I go with no territories but protect key accounts? What about multi-level marketing? Manufacturers' representatives or in-house salespeople versus independent representatives? The various systems of pay and commissions are important decisions that need to be made to sell and distribute any product or service.

Each has its advantages, and each has its drawbacks. A well-thought-out system is important. The only thing worse than regular employees are salespeople. Sorry, but it's true. If there is a quirk in your system, they will find it. Then they will analysis it, take advantage of it, fight over it, and think up ways to change it. Your pricing structure and its various levels need to take into account your commission structure and its various levels of incentive. Your customers' desire for discounts, quantity price breaks, and the like also need to fit this plan.

Certainly, the questions regarding product sales raise more questions than they answer. My main point is to let you know that this part of your business may require an entire plan of its own. No matter how skilled or how wonderful your service or product is, the market needs to know it exists and that it is a viable option. How you get that message out could make all the difference to your success or failure. Success needs to occur before Capital is exhausted by bad decisions or poor planning.

CHAPTER 17

Real Estate and Other Terms

At some time or another, whether in your personal or business life, you are bound to be involved with Real Estate. You will either rent, buy, lease, or sell it at some point. So knowing some of the basic terms and considerations can only aid in your business knowledge and experience. Again, many books out there specialize in telling you how to best buy or sell Real Estate or invest in it. In this chapter, I am only going to try to familiarize you with some of the general terms used by the usual parties to these transactions.

Real Estate brokers and salesmen are licensed individuals who usually represent either the property owner or the buyer. At times, each party has its own agent. A single broker can only have one party's main interest at heart, so it is good to remain aware if you are looking to purchase. The seller's broker is his agent and not yours, no matter how kind or fair they appear. Likewise, if you go to a Real Estate agent to help you search for the right property, he should have your interests first. But remember that he only gets paid if he aids in a sale, so bear that in mind.

Other licensed or professional parties involved may include attorneys, for either side or the bank if one is involved, mortgage brokers, bankers, recorders, and Title Company agents.

Although in many cases it may be wise or even advisable to use a licensed professional, there is no legal requirement to do so. If you own property you may sell it, and if you want to purchase it you may buy it for yourself or your company without being licensed.

All states have a system of recording Real Estate transactions; depending on the state, Recording may occur at the town, city, county, or state level of government. Often this office will be called the Registry of Deeds, the County Recorder's Office, or a similar title. This Registry keeps track of who owns or has Title to each property within its jurisdiction. It records all the changes from one owner to the next and maintains a record of the chain of that history. The Registry also records Liens and Encumbrances against any particular property and owner. These are such things as Mortgages, Judgments, or other claims such as Mechanic's Liens, Lis Pendens, and Easements.

All of these are partial interests against the property by parties other than the owner. For example, if you own a house but take a mortgage loan from a bank, the banker will record a notice with the Recorder. This will make any potential buyer or future lender know that the property is not free and clear to be sold or borrowed against without first satisfying the banker's claim.

Each Recorder's Office keeps records that are public and that can be researched for this information. These offices index books in various ways. You can search by address, by Grantor (person conveying), by Grantee (person conveyed to), and sometimes by other means.

Another office usually found within or very nearby to the

Recorder's Office is that of the Title Company. The Title Company is a business that will perform Title history searches. The company offers an opinion on how certain it is about a property's current ownership, history of transactions, and the probability of an unknown claimant stepping forward to make a claim against a property. For example, a home was left by a Will to certain parties and one of them was never found and told of their interest. The party that is found sells that property but a possible claim exists by the unfound party, who may step forward in the future and assert that he would never have sold his interest had he known of it. Title Companies will also offer Title Insurance for a fee. So if they claim the Title is sound (good) and it turns out later that an interested party has a claim, the Insurance will cover any damages or loss caused by the purchaser relying on the company's search.

There are several types of Title, each conveying various types of rights or interest in the Real Estate. The first and highest form of Title is "Allodial," largely unknown or even heard of today. Being unalienable (un-lien-able) and non-taxable, it began with a Grant of the Sovereign. Originally, this was the Almighty, but in the case of America, it was the King of England to the original 13 colonies after the war for independence. After this level of Title is the Land Patent, granted by the U.S. government to settlers who moved out of the original colonies to form homesteads in the vast lands being acquired by the United States via purchase, claim, and conquest. Like the Allodial, the Land Patent is also largely forgotten today due to the move away from unalienable rights and absolute ownership.

The highest form of Title enjoyed by Real Estate owners (so-called) is to hold Title in "Fee Simple." Fee Simple is thought of today as full ownership, with no encumbrances and the complete Right, Title, and Interest to the property. However, the fact of ever-increasing property taxes and a quick visit to a dictionary should help explain the truth of the matter. The word "Fee" in "Fee Simple" is derived from the word "Fiefdom" or "Fief," meaning of a "Feudal Estate." The Feudal Estate was the land of the Lords who leased it out to serfs for a fee. This becomes more evident when we learn that the other Title types include the word "Tenant."

For instance, some states have Title classification for married couples called "Tenants by the Entirety," where both are considered to own the whole. Title by "Joint Tenancy" is where two or more persons own the whole, with Rights of Survivorship. In contrast, "Tenants in Common" is where two or more persons each own their percentage of the whole and can transfer and pass their share individually as they see fit.

The Rights, Title, and Interest conveyed by these Title types are passed from one person to another by "Deeds," which are recorded by the County Recorder's Office and Searched and Insured for a fee by Title Companies. A "Warranty Deed" is a deed claiming and certifying that the maker has full authority to pass Title to the property and that there are no encumbrances or claims by others. A "Quit Claim Deed," on the other hand, is a deed that claims to give all Right, Title, and Interest of the maker to whomever he is transferring his claim. This Deed, however, does not guarantee the lack of other claims or encumbrances that may exist. In many areas, the purchaser of property receives the Deed to the property immediately, even if a loan is the method of securing the property. The loan then represents a Lien or Encumbrance against the new owner's Interests. In certain areas of the country, a "Contract for Deed" is popular. In this case, the buyer makes payments against a contract that obligates the current owner to transfer Title only after all loan payments have been made by the buyer, who then receives the actual Deed.

"Clouded" or "Cloudy Title" is a term you may hear in connection with property that has Title problems. This state or situation can arise from improper recording, inheritance disputes, prior fraud, or any number of reasons such as my earlier example of the missing heir. Title considered to be "Cloudy" may make a property difficult to sell or transfer. If a Title Company will not Insure the property, most banks will not loan or make mortgages against it, which severely limits the pool of buyers.

When there are disputes over property or Cloudy Title exists, you may have to apply to a court in an action to "Quiet Title." A Quiet Title action is undertaken in hopes that the Court will agree with the application of the party making it as to their claim of complete ownership, and that a favorable ruling will serve to "un-cloud" the Title and cause the Title Company to once again feel secure in its issuance of Title Insurance.

Encumbrances are claims against a property and its clear Title. In an effort to get paid, a party with a claim against another can attempt to get a "Judgment" against the party owning property. The Court then decides whether to award the judgment. Judgments are typically good for up to 20 years or until satisfied, whichever occurs first. Another Encumbrance, usually voluntary, that can occur in the case of a Mortgage is the "Lien." Liens are placed by parties to whom the property owner has pledged payment of a particular debt and has used the value of their Real Property to guarantee it. Liens can also come into play with Home Equity Credit Lines. Similarly, the "Mechanic's Lien" can occur when contracting with construction companies, carpenters, plumbers, or other parties to improve or repair the property of the owner.

Those of you in these types of businesses should be aware of the laws in your particular jurisdiction. Some jurisdictions state that such work automatically warrants a "Mechanic's Lien," while others require the homeowner to first agree to said Lien in writing. If you are in a state where the homeowner must first agree you will want to have Invoices, Estimates, or Quotes with appropriate language securing such agreement before the work begins. Be aware that in cases of husband and wife as "Joint Tenants" on the Deed, both signatures will be required to constitute a claim against the property. So even if, as the contractor, you deal with one or the other to obtain the work you may need both to agree to perfect a Lien. Also, be aware that many people rent and live in homes they do not own; be sure your customer is actually the homeowner and if not get the owners' approval to alter or improve the property. In most places, this is as easy as a trip to the local Town Hall to see the clerk and read the index card on the property address.

A "Lis Pendens" is an unadjudicated or disputed Lien claim against a property. It is a Public Notice and although not a perfected Lien or Judgment, it makes you aware that a claim is pending that may trump any subsequent claim about to be made or affect your receipt of clear Title should you make the purchase.

Tax Liens by various taxing agencies may come after Judgment or Lien or by application of statute, depending on the type of tax and jurisdiction. Other Tax Liens such as an IRS "Notice of Levy" is not a perfected Lien against any Real Property. Although they would like you to believe otherwise, it is more of a Lis Pendens or Public Notice placed at the Recorder's office. It is an unadjudicated claim against particular individuals who may or may not own property in the jurisdiction. It serves the IRS's purposes to scare off potential buyers or to cause attorneys and bankers to think they are required to hold aside the disputed tax amount in escrow for the agency. Hence, the word *Lien* for them can be a license to lie(n). Nonetheless, their tactics serve to bring about a Clouded Title and cause settlement before Title transfer.

An easement is a type of Right or Interest in a property held by someone other than the Titled owner. Such Rights that are secured or agreed upon, even by past owners, remain valid after sale or transfer of the property. Easements may include such things as your neighbor having a Right to share your driveway to get to his otherwise landlocked property. It may be for a utility company's electric lines, gas pipe, or phone cables to pass over or under your land.

A trend in some areas and developments is the "Covenant Deed," or "Restricted Use Deed," on property ownership. Many pre-planned developments and communities are sold with a so-called Covenant Deed. This means that although a purchaser becomes the owner of the Deeded property, the Deed itself does not convey the Right for them to do as they please with their property. In an effort to assure purchasers of certain lifestyles and other preferences that any changes their neighbors might make will not be completely contrary to them, they agree to property restrictions on their Deed. These restrictions and agreements may refer, for example, to how high a home or other structure on the property can be. They may include approved paint colors, home styles, fence heights, and landscape conditions. Some even restrict the number and age of occupants, such as 55-and-over retirement communities. Covenant Deeds are often found today when properties with associations are involved. If that is your thing, great; you can be comfortable knowing you have a hand in controlling your neighbors and vice versa. If it is not your thing, then beware of it today when looking to purchase. Either way, realize you can only sell or pass on those Property Rights that you acquire in the first place.

"Homestead" is another term homeowners and business owners should be aware of. Various states have Acts or Laws protecting individuals from losing their primary home to Creditors. These Laws allow residents to declare their primary residence as their homestead and shield it from Creditors up to a designated amount. Remember also, as previously stated, that when a husband and wife are Joint Tenants on a home, both must sign and agree to any debt encumbering the proper-ty that a Creditor might try to collect.

Another Deed option for the transferring of a property is the reservation of a "Life Estate." Used properly at the right times, this can be a good Estate Planning tool. By naming a person or retaining a Life Estate on a Deed you pass all Right, Title, and Interest in a property to the new Deedholder. However, you reserve the Right to live on the property until death, when complete ownership will pass to the Deedholder.

The person with a Life Estate is usually responsible for property tax, but nothing else. He is required to maintain occupancy and cannot rent out the property or assign his Rights to someone else. On the other hand, the person cannot lose the property to Creditors or suitors—even if he goes bankrupt—as he no longer the owner of the asset. Concerning qualification for Medicaid or other state or federal benefits, however, the Life Estate may be assigned a value against look-back periods and other calculations.

Even more popular than Trusts for running a business are Trusts for holding Real Estate. Real Estate Investment Trusts are businesses for investors, but many small family Trusts hold single properties. As stated previously, these can be Revocable or Irrevocable or even a combination of the two, with timing options written into the Trust Indenture. When deciding between the types, you should take into consideration future plans and goals. Although Irrevocable Trusts offer greater asset protection, they are not reversible; hence they are Irrevocable. If you are sure about your intentions, they are great tools. If you are unsure, they are to be avoided or very carefully designed.

As stated, Trusts can help property be grandfathered against zoning and other regulation changes by avoiding the need to transfer ownership by Deed. The Trust that remains the constant owner may still transfer control by changes of Trustee and Beneficial Interests, which are private property and may avoid public disclosure. Both personal and income properties can be managed privately, and transfer costs and other issues can be avoided through the creative use of perpetual Corporations and Stockholder Trusts.

Although Cloudy Title is usually to be avoided, Trusts can

aid in the ability to use a Clouded Title to one's advantage in the case of adversarial lawsuits. Since the Trust has the attribute of dividing ownership interest into Legal, Equitable, and Beneficial Title, in a court action a suit against one party gives interest and standing to multiple parties. If mishandled, a Trust can serve to Cloud Title for the suitor or interested purchaser of a judgment action.

Even before the acquisition of Real Property, Corporate and Trust containers are easily created entities that can be available and waiting. In the case of a Trust, a container can hold as little as $21 and a signed agreement; with a Corporation, the amount can be as low as $100. This action can set the Incorporation date early and hold a favorable name for later use.

A few words here on Elder Law may be appropriate. In this era of Socialist taxation, the state and multinational corporations in the medical industry frown on passing wealth from one generation to the next and have created many schemes to part you from your money before you can pass it on at death. The days of the old-school method of transferring Deeds to the oldest son shortly before death are gone. Such methods today can be legally dangerous. In fact, older parents could find themselves put out if the son is sued or gets a divorce. Even if these were not issues, the state has created what is referred to as Civil Fraudulent Conveyance Laws. Even with no intent to deceive anyone, just the sheer timing of transactions can cause them to be deemed fraudulent. If within three years of giving property away to family or within five years of settling a Trust you then need costly medical care or government assistance, the value of those transfers could be considered returned to your estate and make you responsible for payment of those amounts. Therefore, early planning is essential. That is why I suggest business planning and Estate Planning be an ongoing combined consideration, not an end-of-life idea. If you have waited too long and such situations are upon you, I suggest you seek out good, competent advice before making any such transactions.

This book was written to hopefully aid in your business success and to help you be more knowledgeable in relating to and choosing the right professionals for advice and services. As stated previously, no one will be more interested in your success than you. And ultimately, win or lose, you will be the one having the experience. Being able to lay blame elsewhere will not change the outcome. Businesses fail every year. Even very successful people have failed at some time. So don't give up on your goals and dreams because of a failure. *You're not down for the count unless you stay down.*

If you have kept your assets in separate baskets, kept your personal assets to a minimum, and refrained from having your home address, phone number, etc. the same as those of your businesses, then even a business failure need not be more than a temporary setback. Not all business failures require you to file bankruptcy. In fact, such a move should be a last resort and undertaken only after serious consideration. You've heard the old saying, "You can't get blood from a stone." Well, it's true. I'm not advocating beating anyone out of anything. If a business has failed, no assets should return to the owner and all of it should be used to pay off debts. But when XYZ Corporation goes bust and no assets remain to finish paying debts, then XYZ Corporation has gone out of business with no assets, period.

Stockholders have Limited Liability and officers have Limited Liability, and all who dealt with XYZ Corporation knew that. Declaring bankruptcy is to involve the federal courts to oversee it. That means making application on federal forms under penalty of perjury and involving attorneys, Receivers, and judges. No one makes the saying "Making a Federal Case out of it" truer than the Feds themselves.

No one I know has ever gone bankrupt correctly because doing it correctly would mean planning on it, and what honest person plans on going bankrupt? Most people do all they can to the point of stress and worry and ulcers before finally being convinced by others that it is their only choice. The problem at that point is they have usually robbed Peter to pay Paul several times. They have paid people they know better than others first and let impersonal Creditors go without. All these things are part of human nature but are against bankruptcy rules, so preferential payments may be reversed. Personal payment for yourself, a family member, or a friend may be considered fraud whether it actually was or not. If you have never been to Court, you may still believe that this institution is about truth and justice. But take the word of everyone else who has firsthand experience—they are not.

Let us now leave the topic of failure and set your sights on success. Remember, the best way to set goals is through proper planning by asking yourself what you really want and listing the answers. Get good advice and plenty of it. Compare opinions but remember that all choices are yours. All responsibility is yours. Remember, what goes around comes around! The most successful and happy people are those who are grateful, honest, and hard-working. Schemes and a quick buck may seem appealing, but quick bucks disappear just as quickly; remember—easy come, easy go. Quality products and excellent services delivered with integrity is what lasts for the long haul.

The ideas and asset protection techniques I mention in the pages of this book are not to aid anyone in getting over on their neighbor, business associates, or customers; heaven knows, corruption abounds at every turn in our lives today. In my opinion, this country has a major integrity problem. People are happy to become rich today by any means, which is very sad. This country needs men and women of integrity to stand up and say "no" to corruption, "no" to getting ahead by dishonest means. And to say, "I'm not" to those who say, "everybody's doing it."

I hope you will use the information I offer to protect against the corrupt, the sue-happy, and those who want something for nothing. To reduce your tax burdens and benefit the lives of your family and friends. Most of all, I hope you will commit to join the business world as a person of integrity and find blessing in doing and becoming successful by righteous means. In my life, that has meant finally drawing a line in the sand and committing to being obedient to the commands of the Almighty (our heavenly father and his son), as relayed to us in the Ten Commandments. To paraphrase, "Love the Almighty with all your heart and your neighbor as yourself."

APPENDIX A

Secretary of State Websites

Below is a list of the business websites of various states. Most have business name lookup features as well as all the information necessary for doing business within their state. A simple search on Google or any other search engine will net you dozens of options, all with links to referenced locations. Therefore, including long lists here would not serve you any better.

https://businessentity.org/secretary-of-state-business-entity-search/

https://www.llcuniversity.com/50-secretary-of-state-sos-business-entity-search/

https://www.thebalancesmb.com/secretary-of-state-websites-1201005

http://www.coordinatedlegal.com/SecretaryOfState.html

Mortgage, Payroll and Other Calculators

Below are a few of the many websites that list various calculators of all kinds. You can find many free convenient tools on the Internet that are very useful to the small businessperson. A simple search on Google or any other search engine will net you dozens of options, all with links to referenced locations. Find your favorites and bookmark them in your browser for quick access.

Mortgage Calculators:
https://www.mortgagecalculator.org/
https://www.zillow.com/mortgage-calculator/
https://www.mlcalc.com/

Payroll Calculators:
https://www.paycheckcity.com/calculator/salary/
https://www.paycheckmanager.com/FreeCal/free_payroll_calculat
    or.aspx
https://www.adp.com/resources/tools/calculators.aspx
https://quickbooks.intuit.com/r/paycheck-calculator/

Budget Calculators:
https://www.quicken.com/budget-calculator
http://www.youcandealwithit.com/borrowers/calculators-and-
    resources/calculators/budget-calculator.shtml
https://www.calculator.net/budget-calculator.html

Sample Contracts

Sample General Partnership Agreement:

The General Partnership Agreement
of
L & S Gamers,
General Partnership

This Partnership Agreement made effective November 2, 2018, by the following hereinafter known as General Partners:

Steven F. Smith
36 Any Street
Salem, NH 03854

Andrew C. Jones
16 Central Street
Rochester, NH 03855

The said Partners do hereby covenant and agree to the formation of this Partnership and do hereby covenant and agree to be found by these Articles as follows, to-wit: L & S Gamers, General Partnership

Article I

Formation
Name
Principal Place of Business

Section 1.1 Formation. The Partners hereby form a General Partnership pursuant to the provisions of the New Hampshire Law.

Section 1.2 Name. The Partnership shall operate under the name of: L & S Gamers, GP.

Section 1.3 Principal Place of Business. The principal place of business shall be at 16 Central Street, Rochester, NH 03855, with such other places of business as may be agreed upon by the Partners from time to time.

Article II

Term of the Partnership

Section 2.1 Term of the Partnership. The Partnership shall commence on the date hereof and shall continue for twenty-five years unless sooner terminated by law or as hereinafter provided.

Article III

Method of Accounting
Annual Statements
Annual Meeting to Review Financial Statements
Interim Financial Statements

Section 3.1 Method of Accounting. The Partnership shall keep its accounting records on the cash basis. The records shall be maintained in accordance with generally accepted accounting principles.

Section 3.2 Annual Statements. Financial statements shall be prepared not less than annually and copies of the statement shall be delivered to each partner.

Section 3.3 Annual Meeting to Review Financial Statements. Not less than once a year, and as soon as possible after completion of the financial statements, a meeting of the Partners shall be held to review and discuss the financial statements of the Partnership. All annual meetings shall be held at the principal place of business in New Hampshire on the first Thursday in March unless otherwise provided pursuant to actual or constructive notice to each Partner.

Section 3.4 Interim Financial Statements. On written request, each Partner shall be entitled to copies of any interim financial statements prepared for the Partnership.

Article IV

Initial Capital Contributions
Additional Capital Contributions
Return of Capital Contributions

Section 4.1 Initial Capital Contributions. The initial capital contributions shall be as follows:

Steven F. Smith.......................50%

Andrew C. Jones.....................50%

Percentage interests express the share of property or assets contributed by and for the Partners shown on the attached Schedule A.

Section 4.2 Additional Capital Contributions. There shall be no additional capital contributions to the capital of the Partnership unless otherwise agreed to in writing by all of the Partners.

Section 4.3 Return of Capital Contributions. A Partner may assign his interest to others but only as hereinafter provided. No Partner shall be entitled to withdraw or demand the return of any part of their capital contribution except upon dissolution of the Partnership as specifically provided for in this Agreement.

Article V

Capital Accounts
Drawing Accounts

Section 5.1 Capital Accounts. An individual Capital Account may be maintained for each Partner. The capital interest of each Partner shall consist of their original contribution increased by (*a*) his/her additional contributions to capital and (*b*) his/her share of Partnership profits transferred to capital and decreased by (*a*) distributions in reduction of Partnership capital and (*b*) share of Partnership losses if transferred from a drawing account.

Section 5.2 Drawing accounts. An individual drawing account may be maintained for each Partner. All withdrawals made by a Partner shall be charged to a drawing account. Each partner's share of profits and losses shall be credited or charged to their drawing account. A credit balance of a Partner's drawing account shall constitute the Partnership's liability to that Partner; it shall not constitute a part of their Capital Account or their interest in the capital of the Partnership. If, after the net profit or the net loss of the Partnership for the fiscal year has been determined, a Partner's drawing account shows a deficit, whether occasioned by drawings in excess of share of Partnership profits or by a charging of their share of a Partnership loss, the deficit shall constitute an obligation of that Partner to the Partnership to the extent of the Partner's Capital Account. There shall be a requirement to have all Partners' drawing accounts balance on a monthly basis. Upon the occurrence of a deficit at month end in a Partner's drawing account, the amount available to draw during the next month shall be reduced until the deficit is made up. Should any one Partner's drawing account repeatedly show a deficit over any three-month period, it would be construed as a Breach of Contract and handled in accordance with Sec. 9.2 as therein-after provided.

Article VI

Interests in Profits or Losses
Distribution of Profits

Section 6.1 Interests in Profits or Losses. The net profits or net losses of the Partnership shall be credited or charged to the

Partners in proportion to their Partnership interests.

Section 6.2 Distribution of Profits. The earnings of the Partnership shall be distributed at least annually, except that earnings may be retained by the Partnership and transferred to Partnership capital for the reasonable needs of the business as determined by the Partners. There will be no distribution of profits to any Partner for any period of time in which the requirements of Sec. 7.1 are not maintained.

Article VII
Time Devoted by General Partners
Validity
Powers of General Partners

Section 7.1 Time Devoted by General Partners. The Partners are required to devote to the business of the Partnership a minimum of twenty (20) billable, on time, hours per week in order to meet the outside contracts and obligations of the Partnership. Any additional time needed to meet the obligations of the Partnership may be required upon a vote of the Partners.

Section 7.2 Validity. If any portions of this Agreement shall be held invalid or inoperative, then, insofar as it is reasonable and possible, (*a*) the remainder of this Agreement shall be considered valid and operative, and (*b*) effect shall be given to the intent manifested by the portion held invalid or inoperative.

Section 7.3 Powers of the Partners. The Partners shall conduct the business of the Partnership by acting through one or more

Managing General Partner(s). As such, the Managing General Partner(s) shall have and is hereby granted the usual, proper, and necessary authority and powers to manage, control, operate, conduct, and carry on the business of the Partnership; keep the books and records thereof; and have the authority to draw checks and drafts on the Partnership bank accounts. The Managing General Partner(s) shall be under no obligation to spend any of the capital of the Partnership, but may use such portions thereof as he/she deems essential for the best interests of the Partnership. In order to conduct and carry on the general purposes for which this Partnership is organized, the Managing General Partner(s) may borrow money from time to time for and on behalf of this Partnership from any bank, trust company, savings and loan association, life insurance company, or other individuals or lending agencies; may renew and extend such loans from time to time; may make, execute, and deliver promissory notes, endorsements, and other obligations of this Partnership as evidence of any such loans; and may secure the payments of such loans and the interest thereon by the pledge, conveyance, mortgage, or assignment in trust of the whole or any part of the property of this Partnership owned at the time or acquired thereafter.

Article VIII

Hold Harmless
Expenses
Taxes

Section 8.1 Hold Harmless. All Partners agree to hold the Partnership harmless for any health-related injuries whether connected or not to the work of the Partnership. All Partners agree and acknowledge that any one partner is responsible for providing, at that Partner's own expense, disability and all other insurance, training, permits, and licenses should it be desired or necessary for any one partner and/or required by law, if any. As no Private or Personal use is allowed of the Partnership owned/leased vehicles, should any Partner make Private or Personal use of said vehicles he/she shall hold harmless the Partnership.

Section 8.2 Expenses. The Managing General Partner(s) shall review and reimburse all expense records submitted by the Partners for expenses incurred during the operation of the Partnership.

Section 8.3 Tax Liabilities. The Partners agree to make sole and complete determination, and will be responsible, when required by law, for paying all taxes, income and otherwise, incurred as a result of the profits they receive from the Partnership.

Article IX

Duration of Business

Arbitration

Dissolution

In the Event of Dissolution

Section 9.1 Duration of Business. The Partnership shall continue (*a*) until all of the interests in the property acquired by it have been sold, disposed of, or abandoned; or (*b*) until dissolved as provided for herein below.

Section 9.2 Arbitration. The Partnership may terminate the interest of any Partner and expel him (*a*) for actions which could result in the Partnership losing its tax status as a Partnership; (*b*) if the conduct of a Partner tends to bring the Partnership into disrepute or his/her interest becomes subject to attachment, garnishment, or similar legal proceedings; or (*c*) for failing to meet any commitment to the Partnership in accordance with any written undertaking. In each of the foregoing events, the termination shall not result in forfeiture of the value of the Partner's interest in the Partnership at the time of termination.

Section 9.3 Dissolution. The Partnership shall be dissolved only upon the occurrence of any of the following events:

a. The disposition or sale of all interests in real estate and other Partnership assets.

b. The expiration of the time period set forth in Article II.

c. Voluntary dissolution of the Partnership by agreement of the Partners.

d. The entry of a dissolution decree or judicial order by a court of competent jurisdiction or by operation of law.

Section 9.4 In the Event of Dissolution. In the event of dissolution and final termination: The Partners shall wind up the affairs of the Partnership and shall sell all the Partnership assets as promptly as is consistent with obtaining, insofar as is possible, the fair value thereof. And, after paying all liabilities, including all costs of dissolution and also subject to the right of the Partners to set up cash reserves to meet short-term Partnership liabilities, other liabilities, or obligations of the

Partnership, the Partners shall distribute the remainder proportionally pursuant to the relevant provisions of this Agreement.

Article X

Sale

Section 10.1 Sale. **A Partner may sell his Partnership interest, but only after it has first been offered to the Partnership as follows:**

a. The Partner shall give written notice to the Partnership that he desires to sell his interest.

b. For 30 days from receipt of the written notice from the Partner, the Partnership shall have the option to purchase the interest of the Partner. During this time period the value of his interest shall be limited to the value of his Capital Account with the Partnership.

c. If the Partnership does not exercise the option to acquire his/her interest, the Partner shall be free to sell his/her Partnership interest to any other prospective purchaser for any price. The Partners will be required to amend the Agreement of Partnership only quarterly to reflect the substitution of a Partner. Until the Agreement of Partnership is so amended, an assignee shall not become a substituted Partner. Upon the death or incapacity of an individual Partner, his/her personal representative shall have all of the rights of a Partner for the purpose of settling or managing his/her estate. All of Section 10.1 shall apply in handling the settling of the Partner's interest.

Article XI

Voluntary Dissolution

Gains or Losses in Process of Liquidation

Section 11.1 Voluntary Dissolution. On any voluntary dissolution, the Partnership shall immediately commence to wind up its affairs. The Partners shall continue to share profits and losses during the period of liquidation in the same proportions as before dissolution. The proceeds from liquidation of Partnership assets shall be applied as follows:

a. Payment to creditors of the Partnership, other than Partners, in the order of priority provided by law.

b. Payment to Partners for the credit balances in their drawing accounts.

c. Payment to the Partners of credit balances in their Capital Accounts.

Section 11.2 Gains or Losses in Process of Liquidation. Any gain or loss on disposition of Partnership properties in liquidation shall be credited or charged to the Partners in the proportions of their interest in profits or losses, as specified in Section 6.1. Any property distributed in kind in liquidation shall be valued and treated as though the property were sold and the cash proceeds were distributed. The difference between the value of property distributed in kind and its book value shall be treated as a gain or loss on sale of the property and shall be credited or charged to the Partners in the proportions of their interests in profits and losses, as specified in Section 6.1.

Agreed to and accepted by:

_____

Steven F. Smith, *General Partner*

_____

Andrew C. Jones, *General Partner*

Sample Limited Partnership Agreement:

Limited Partnership Agreement
of
Acme Property Management, Limited Partnership

A New Hampshire Limited Partnership

This Limited Partnership Agreement made effective October 5, 2018, by the following hereinafter known as General Partner:

Anne M. Smith

and by the following hereinafter referred to as Limited Partners:

Jones Family Trust

The said Partners do hereby covenant and agree to the formation of this Limited Partnership and do hereby covenant and agree to be bound by these Articles as follows, to-wit:

Article I

Formation

Name

Principal Place of Business

Section 1.1 Formation. The Partners hereby form a Limited Partnership pursuant to the provisions of the New Hampshire State Limited Partnership Act. The Partners shall execute and cause to be filed a Certificate of Limited Partnership as required by New Hampshire law.

Section 1.2 Name. The Partnership shall operate under the name of: Acme Property Management, Limited Partnership.

Section 1.3 Principal Place of Business. The principal place of business shall be at 5 Elm Street, Rochester, New Hampshire, with such other places of business as may be agreed upon by the Partners from time to time.

Article II

Term of the Partnership

Section 2.1 Term of the Partnership. The Partnership shall commence on the date hereof and shall continue for twenty-five years unless sooner as terminated by law or as hereinafter provided.

Article III

Method of Accounting
Annual Statements
Annual Meeting to Review Financial Statements
Interim Financial Statements

Section 3.1 Method of Accounting. The Partnership shall keep its accounting records and shall make any required reports for income tax purposes on the cash basis. The records shall be maintained in accordance with generally accepted accounting principles.

Section 3.2 Annual Statements. Financial statements shall be prepared not less than annually and copies of the statements shall be delivered to each partner. Copies of all required income tax returns filed by the Partnership shall also be furnished to all Partners.

Section 3.3 Annual Meeting to Review Financial Statements. Not less than once a year, and as soon as possible after completion of the financial statements, a meeting shall be held of all General and Limited Partners. The meeting shall include discussion and review of the financial statements thereby reporting to the Limited Partners the financial condition of Acme Property Management, Limited Partnership. All annual meetings shall be held at the principal place of business in Rochester, New Hampshire, on the first Tuesday in July unless otherwise provided pursuant to actual or constructive notice to each General and Limited Partner.

Section 3.4 Interim Financial Statements. On written request, any Limited Partner shall be entitled to copies of any interim financial statements prepared for the General Partners.

Article IV

Initial Capital Contributions

Respective Interests of Partners in the Initial Capital Contribution

Additional Capital Contributions

Return of Capital Contributions

Section 4.1 Initial Capital Contributions. The initial capital contributions shall be as follows:

General Partner

Anne M. Smith......................20%

Limited Partners

Jones Family Trust.....................80%

Percentage interests express the share of property shown on the attached Schedule A contributed by and for the Partners.

Section 4.2 Respective Interests of Partners in the Initial Capital Contribution. The interests of the Partners in the Capital originally contributed are the same as those listed above.

Section 4.3 Additional Capital Contributions. There shall be no additional Capital contributions to the Capital of the Partnership unless otherwise agreed to in writing by all of the Partners. A Limited Partner or a General Partner may assign his/her interest to others but only as hereinafter provided.

Section 4.4 Return of Capital Contributions. No Limited Partner shall be entitled to withdraw or demand the return of any part of his Capital contribution except upon dissolution of the Partnership as specifically provided for in this Agreement.

Article V
Capital Accounts
Drawing Accounts

Section 5.1 Capital Accounts. An individual Capital Account shall be maintained for each General and Limited Partner. The Capital interest of each General and Limited Partner shall consist of his/her original contribution increased by (*a*) his/her additional contributions to capital and (*b*) his/her share of Partnership profits transferred to capital and decreased by (*a*) distributions to him/her in reduction of his/her Partnership capital and (*b*) his/her share of Partnership losses if transferred from his/her drawing account.

Section 5.2 Drawing Accounts. An individual drawing account shall be maintained for each General and Limited Partner. All withdrawals, other than salaries, made by a General or Limited Partner shall be charged to his/her drawing account. Each partner's share of profits and losses shall be credited or charged to his/her drawing account. A credit balance of a Partner's drawing account shall constitute a Partnership liability to that Partner; it shall not constitute a part of his/her Capital Account or his/her interest in the Capital of the Partnership. If, after the net profit or the net loss of the Partnership for the fiscal year has been determined, a Partner's drawing account shows a deficit (a debit balance), whether occasioned by drawings in excess of his share of Partnership profits or by charging him/her for his/her share of a Partnership loss, the deficit shall constitute an obligation of that Partner to the Partnership to the extent of the Partner's Capital Account, but in no event shall any Limited Partner be liable for any amount beyond the balance in his Capital Account. Payment of any amount owing to the Partnership shall be made in a manner and at a time determined by the General Partners. Such obligations shall not be made payable on demand nor shall interest be charged thereon above the prime interest rate plus 3 percentage points. The Limited Partners may determine by vote of a majority in interest to transfer any portion of their respective profit or loss to their Capital Accounts at any time provided the transfers do not change the Partners' respective Partnership interests except by written consent of all Partners.

Article VI

Interests in Profits or Losses
Limitation on Liability for Losses Chargeable to Limited Partners
Distribution of Profits

Section 6.1 Interests in Profits or Losses. The net profits or net losses of the Partnership shall be credited or charged to the Partners in proportion to their Partnership interests (generally construed as the Capital Account).

Section 6.2 Limitation on Liability for Losses Chargeable to Limited Partners. No Limited Partner shall be personally liable for any of the losses of the Partnership beyond his/her Capital interest in the Partnership.

Section 6.3 Distribution of Profits. The earnings of the Partnership shall be distributed at least annually except that earnings may be retained by the Partnership and transferred to Partnership Capital for the reasonable needs of the business as determined by the sole discretion of the General Partners.

Article VII

Management
Time Devoted by General Partners
Banking
Validity
Indemnification
Powers of General Partners

Section 7.1 Management. The business of the Partnership shall be under the exclusive control of the General Partners who shall act by a majority vote in all business affairs. For these purposes each General Partner shall have one vote. The Limited Partners shall not participate in the management of the business of the Partnership.

Section 7.2 Time Devoted by General Partners. The General Partners are required to devote to the business of the Partnership such time as is reasonable and prudent.

Section 7.3 Banking. All funds in the Partnership shall be deposited in its name in such checking account or accounts as shall be designated by the General Partners. All withdrawals therefrom shall be made upon checks signed by at least one (1) of the General Partners. A General Partner shall have all the rights and powers, and be subject to all the restrictions and liabilities, of a Partner in a Partnership without Limited Partners, except that without the written consent or ratification of the specific act by all the Limited Partners, a General Partner or all of the General Partners have no authority that is specifically denied them according to the New Hampshire Limited Partnership Act.

Section 7.4 Validity. If any portions of this Agreement shall be held invalid or inoperative, then, insofar as it is reasonable and possible, (*a*) the remainder of this Agreement shall be considered valid and operative and (*b*) effect shall be given to the intent manifested by the portion held invalid or inoperative.

Section 7.5 Indemnification. The Partnership shall promptly indemnify each Partner for payments reasonably made and personal liabilities reasonably incurred by him/her in the ordinary conduct of Partnership business or for the preservation of its business or property.

Section 7.6 Powers of General Partners. The General Partners shall conduct the business of the Limited Partnership with full and complete power to do any and all things, including acting through a Managing General Partner or through any duly authorized manager or other agent, except as otherwise provided herein; and the General Partners shall use their reasonable efforts to provide that each Limited Partner has the full enjoyment of its Partnership interest. Such General Partners shall have and are hereby granted the usual, proper, and necessary authority and powers to manage, control, operate, conduct, and carry on the business of the Partnership; keep the books and records thereof; employ, discharge, and compensate necessary employees, clerks, and helpers; and have the authority to draw checks and drafts on the Partnership bank accounts. The General Partners shall be under no obligation to spend any of the capital of the Limited Partnership, but they may use such portions thereof as they deem essential for the best interests of the Partnership. The General Partners may by agreement grant, assign, transfer, lease, or let any of the property of the Limited Partners, whether real or personal, in furtherance of the business of the Partnership and, in connection therewith, may execute in the Partnership's name any and all deeds, documents, bills of sale, and other papers pertaining to the business of the Partnership. In order to conduct and carry on the general purposes for which this Limited Partnership is organized, the General Partners may borrow money from time to time for and on behalf of this Limited Partnership from any bank, trust company, savings and loan association, life insurance company, or other individuals or lending agencies; may renew and extend such loans from time to time; may make, execute, and deliver promissory notes, endorsements, and other obligations of this Partnership as evidence of any such loans; and may secure the payments of such loans and the interest thereon by the pledge, conveyance, mortgage, or assignment in trust of the whole or any part of the property of this Partnership owned at the time or acquired thereafter.

Article VIII
Original Salary

Section 8.1 Original Salary. Annually, the General Partners shall each receive a reasonable salary for services rendered, which shall be in addition to their respective share of Partnership profits. It is the intention of the parties that each General Partner shall receive reasonable compensation for services rendered by him/her to the Partnership. His/her compensation shall be reviewed periodically and adjusted.

Article IX
Duration of Business
Termination
Arbitration
Removal
Dissolution
In the Event of Dissolution

Section 9.1 Duration of Business. The Limited Partnership shall continue (*a*) until all of the interests in the property acquired by it have been sold, disposed of, or abandoned or (*b*) until dissolved and terminated as provided for herein below.

Section 9.2 Termination. The Limited Partnership shall not be terminated by the death, insanity, bankruptcy, or withdrawal of any Limited Partner; nor by the assignment by any Limited Partner of his interest or by the admission of a new Limited Partner or admission of an additional General Partner.

Section 9.3 Arbitration. The General Partners may terminate the interest of a Limited Partner and expel him/her (*a*) for interfering in the management of the Limited Partnership affairs or other actions which could result in the Limited Partnership losing its tax status as a Partnership; (*b*) if his/her conduct tends to bring the Limited Partnership into disrepute or his interest becomes subject to attachment, garnishment, or similar legal proceedings; or (*c*) for failing to meet any commitment to the General Partner in accordance with any written undertaking. In each of the foregoing events, the termination shall not result in a forfeiture to the Limited Partner of the value of his interest(s) in the Partnership at the time of termination.

Section 9.4 Removal. Upon the written consent or affirmative vote of Limited Partners owning 89% of the then-outstanding Partnership interests, the General Partner may be removed if, simultaneously with such removal, a successor General Partner is elected by the Limited Partners owning 89% of the then-outstanding Partnership interest.

Section 9.5 Dissolution. The Limited Partnership shall be dissolved only upon the occurrence of any of the following events: a. The written consent or affirmative vote to dissolve the Limited Partnership of Limited Partners owning more than 89% of the then-outstanding Partnership interests. b. The failure to elect a successor to the General Partner simultaneously with the removal of the General Partner in accordance with Section 9.4. c. Bankruptcy or dissolution (except by way of merger, consolidation, corporate organization or reorganization, death, insanity, or retirement of the surviving General

Partner) provided that in any such event the Limited Partners owning more than 50% of the then-outstanding Partnership interests may determine to re-form the Limited Partnership and elect a new General Partner in place of the General Partner and continue the Partnership's business; in such event, the Limited Partnership shall be dissolved and all of its assets and liabilities shall be contributed to a new Limited Partnership which shall be formed and all parties to this Agreement (except the General Partner) and such new General Partner shall become parties to such new Limited Partnership. For purposes of obtaining the required vote to re-form the Partnership, Limited Partners owning 10% or more of the then-outstanding Partnership interests may cause to be sent to the Limited Partners of record, as of a date no more than 20 days prior to the date fixed by such Limited Partners for holding a Partnership meeting, a notice setting forth the purpose of the meeting. Expenses incurred in the reformation or attempted reformation of the Partnership shall be deemed expenses of the Limited Partnership. The disposition or sale of all interests in real estate and other Partnership assets. e. The expiration of the time period set forth in Article II. f. Voluntary dissolution of the Partnership by agreement of the Partners. g. The entry of a dissolution decree or judicial order by a court of competent jurisdiction or by operation of law.

Section 9.6 In the Event of Dissolution. In the event of dissolution and final termination: The General Partners shall wind up the affairs of the Limited Partnership and shall sell all the Limited Partnership assets as promptly as is consistent with obtaining, insofar as is possible, the fair value thereof. And, after paying all liabilities, including all costs of dissolution and also subject to the right of the General Partners to set up cash reserves to meet short-term Partnership liabilities, other liabilities, or obligations of the Limited Partnership, shall distribute the remainder proportionally to the Partners pursuant to the relevant provisions of this Agreement.

Article X

Sale

Substituted Limited Partner

Section 10.1 Sale. A Limited Partner may sell his/her Partnership interest, but only after he/she has first offered it to the Partnership as follows: a. The Limited Partner shall give written notice to the Partnership that he/she desires to sell his/her interest. He shall attach to that notice the written offer of a prospective purchaser to buy the interest. This offer shall be complete in all details of purchase price and terms of payment. The Limited Partner shall certify that the offer is genuine and in all respects what it purports to be. b. For 120 days from receipt of the written notice from the Limited Partner, the Partnership shall have the option to retire the interest of the Limited Partner at the price and on the terms contained in the offer submitted by the Limited Partner. c. If the Partnership does not exercise the option to acquire his interest, the Limited Partner shall be free to sell his Partnership interest to the said prospective purchaser for the price, and on the terms contained in the certified offer submitted by the Limited Partners without the consent of any other Limited Partner.

Section 10.2 Substituted Limited Partner. No assignee or transferee of the whole or any portion of a Limited Partner's interest in the Limited Partnership shall have the right to become a substituted Limited Partner in place of his assignor unless all of the following conditions are satisfied: a. The General Partner, in its sole and absolute discretion, has consented in writing to the admission of the assignee as a substituted Limited Partner. b. The fully executed and acknowledged written instrument of assignment which has been filed with the Limited Partnership sets forth the intention of the assignor that the assignee become a substitute Limited Partner, c. The Limited Partnership interest being acquired by the assignee consists of 100% of the assigning Limited Partner's interest. d. The assignor and assignee execute and acknowledge such other instruments as the General Partner may deem necessary or desirable to effect such admission, including the written acceptance and adoption by the assignee of the provisions of this Agreement and his/her execution, acknowledgment, and delivery to the General Partner of a Power of Attorney—the form and content of which shall be provided by the General Partner. e. A transfer fee of $20,000 has been paid by the assignee to the Limited Partnership. The General Partner may elect to treat an assignee who has not become a substituted Limited Partner as a substituted Limited Partner in the place of his assignor should it deem, in its sole discretion, that such treatment is in the best interest of the Limited Partnership for any of its purposes or for any of the purposes of this Agreement. No consent of any of the Limited Partners is required to effect the substitution of a Limited Partner, except that a Limited Partner who assigns his/her interest must evidence his/her intention that his/her assignee be admitted as a substituted Limited Partner in his place and execute any instruments required in connection therewith. The General Partner will be required to amend the Agreement of Limited Partnership only quarterly to reflect the substitution of Limited Partners. Until the Agreement of Limited Partnership is so amended, an assignee shall not become a substituted Limited Partner. Upon the death or incapacity of an individual Limited Partner, his/her personal representative shall have all of the rights of a Limited Partner for the purpose of settling or managing his/her estate and such power as the decedent or incompetent possesses to constitute a successor as an assignee of its interest in the Limited Partnership and to join with such assignee in making application to substitute such assignee as a Limited Partner. Upon the bankruptcy, insolvency, dissolution, or other circumstance causing cessation as a legal entity of a Limited Partner (not an individual), the authorized representative of such entity shall have all the rights of a Limited Partner for the purpose of effecting the orderly winding up and disposition of the business of such entity and such power as such entity possessed to constitute a successor as an assignee of its interest in the Limited Partnership and to join with such assignee in making application to substitute such assignee as a Limited Partner. Anything in this Agreement to the contrary notwithstanding, no Limited Partner or other person who has become the holder of interests in this Limited Partnership shall transfer, assign, or encumber all or any portion of his interests in the Limited Partnership during any fiscal year if such transfer, assignment, or encumbrance would (in the sole and unreviewable opinion of the General Partner) result in the termination of the Partnership for purposes of the then-applicable provisions of the Internal Revenue Code of 1954, as amended. In the event a vote of the Limited Partners shall be taken pursuant to this Agreement for any reason, a Limited Partner shall, solely for the purpose of determining the number of Partnership interests held by him/her in weighing his/her vote, be deemed the holder of any Partnership interests assigned by him/her in respect of which the assignee has not become a substituted Limited Partner. Anything in this Agreement to the contrary notwithstanding, no Limited Partner or other person who has become the holder of interests in the Partnership shall transfer, assign, or encumber all or any portion of his/her interests in the Limited Partnership unless obtaining the prior written consent of the Director of the Securities Commission, if required under the Commission's rules and the opinion of counsel for the Partnership so that the transfer will not violate any federal or applicable State securities laws.

Article XI

Voluntary Dissolution
Gains or Losses in Process of Liquidation

Section 11.1 Voluntary Dissolution. On any voluntary dissolution, the Partnership shall immediately commence to wind up its affairs. The Partners shall continue to share profits and losses during the period of liquidation in the same proportions as before dissolution. The proceeds from liquidation of Partnership assets shall be applied as follows: a. Payment to creditors of the Partnership, other than Partners, in the order of priority provided by law. b. Payment to Partners for unpaid salaries and for the credit balances in their drawing accounts. c. Payment to the Partners of credit balances in their Capital Accounts.

Section 11.2 Gains or Losses in Process of Liquidation. Any gain or loss on disposition of Partnership properties in liquidation shall be credited or charged to the Partners in the proportions of their interest in profits or losses as specified in Section 6.1. Any property distributed in kind in liquidation shall be valued and treated as though the property were sold and the cash proceeds were distributed. The difference between the value of property distributed in kind and its book value shall be treated as a gain or loss on sale of the property and shall be credited or charged to the Partners in the proportions of their interests in profits and losses as specified in Section 6.1.

Article XII
Amendments

Section 12.1 Amendments. Except with respect to vested rights of the Partners, this Partnership Agreement may be amended at any time by a majority vote as measured by the interest in the sharing of profits and losses. A copy of any amendment shall be promptly mailed or delivered to each Partner at his/her last known address.

Article XIII
Power of Attorney

Section 13.1 Power of Attorney. Each Limited Partner makes, constitutes, and appoints the General Partners, with full power of substitution, his true and lawful attorneys for him and in his name, place., and stead, and for his use and benefit to sign, execute, certify, acknowledge, file, and record this Agreement and to sign, execute, certify, acknowledge, file, and record all appropriate instruments amending this Agreement as now hereafter amended, including, without limitation, agreements or other instruments or documents: (*a*) to reflect the exercise by the General Partners of any of the powers granted to them under this Agreement; (*b*) to reflect any amendments duly made to the Agreement; and (*c*) to reflect the admission to the Partnership of a substituted Limited Partner or the withdrawal of any Partner, in the manner prescribed in this Agreement. Each Limited Partner authorizes such attorneys-in-fact to take any further action which such attorneys-in-fact shall consider necessary or advisable to be done in and about the foregoing (including the power to consent to items (*a*), (*b*), and (*c*) above as fully as such Limited Partner might or could do if personally present and hereby ratifies and confirms all that such attorney-in-fact shall lawfully do or cause to be done by virtue hereof.

Anne M. Smith, *General Partner*

Jones Family Trust, *Limited Partner*

Sample Limited Liability Company (LLC):

LIMITED LIABILITY COMPANY AGREEMENT
of
ABC, LLC

This Limited Liability Company Agreement (the "Agreement") made and entered into this _____ day of _____, _____ (the "Execution Date"),

BETWEEN:

John Doe of 34 Oak Street, Hudson, NH 03051, and

Jones Family Trust of 12 Haven Drive, Hudson, NH 03051

(individually the "Member" and collectively the "Members").

BACKGROUND:

A. The Members wish to associate themselves as members of a limited liability company.

B. The terms and conditions of this Agreement will govern the Members within the limited liability company.

IN CONSIDERATION OF and as a condition of the Members entering into this Agreement and other valuable consideration, the receipt and sufficiency of which is acknowledged, the Members agree as follows:

<u>Formation</u>

1. By this Agreement, the Members form a Limited Liability Company (the "Company") in accordance with the laws of the State of New Hampshire. The rights and obligations of the Members will be as stated in Chapter 304-C of the New

Hampshire Revised Statutes (the "Act") except as otherwise provided in this agreement.

Name

2. The name of the Company will be ABC, LLC.

Purpose

3. Reglazing and other construction maintenance and repair.

Term

4. The Company will continue until terminated as provided in this Agreement or may dissolve under conditions provided in the Act.

Place of Business

5. The Principal Office of the Company will be located at 5 Main Street, Nashua, NH 03060 or such other place as the Members may from time to time designate.

Capital Contributions

6. The following is a list of all Members and their Initial Contributions to the Company. Each of the Members agree to make their Initial Contributions to the Company in full, according to the following terms:

Member	Contribution Description	Value of Contribution
John Doe		$_____
Jones Family Trust		$_____

Allocation of Profits/Losses

7. Subject to the other provisions of this Agreement, the Net Profits or Losses, for both accounting and tax purposes, will be allocated between the Members in the following manner:

Member	Profit/Loss Percentage
John Doe	51.00%
Jones Family Trust	49.00%

8. Distributions to Members will be made in the same fixed proportions as the allocation of Net Profits or Losses described above.

9. No Member will have priority over any other Member for the distribution of Net Profits or Losses.

Nature of Interest

10. A Member's Interest in the Company will be considered personal property.

Withdrawal of Contribution

11. No Member will withdraw any portion of their Capital Contribution without the unanimous consent of the other Members.

Liability for Contribution

12. A Member's obligation to make their required Capital Contribution can only be compromised or released with the consent of all remaining Members or as otherwise provided in this Agreement. If a Member does not make the Capital Contribution when it is due, he is obligated at the option of

any remaining Members to contribute cash equal to the agreed value of the Capital Contribution. This option is in addition to and not in lieu of any others' rights, including the right to specific performance that the Company may have against the Member.

Additional Contributions

13. No Member will be required to make Additional Contributions. Any changes to Capital Contributions will not affect any Member's Interests except with the unanimous consent of the Members.

14. Any advance of money to the Company by any Member in excess of the amounts provided for in this Agreement, or subsequently agreed to, will be deemed a debt due from the Company rather than an increase in the Capital Contribution of the Member. This liability will be repaid with interest at such rates and times to be determined by a majority of the Members. This liability will not entitle the lending Member to any increased share of the Company's profits nor to a greater voting power. Repayment of such debts will have priority over any other payments to Members.

Capital Accounts

15. An individual Capital Account (the "Capital Account") will be maintained for each Member and their Initial Contributions will be credited to this account. Any Additional Contributions made by any Member will be credited to that Member's individual Capital Account.

Interest on Capital

16. No borrowing charge or loan interest will be due or payable to any Member on their agreed Capital Contribution inclusive of any agreed Additional Contributions.

Management

17. Management of this Company is vested in the Members.

Authority to Bind Company

18. Only the following individuals, classes, or groups have authority to bind the Company in contract: Managing Member only.

Duty of Loyalty

19. While a person is a Member of the Company, and for a period of at least two years after that person ceases to be a Member, that person will not carry on, or participate in, a similar business to the business of the Company within any market regions that were established or contemplated by the Company before or during that person's tenure as Member.

Duty to Devote Time

20. Each Member will devote such time and attention to the business of the Company as the majority of the Members will from time to time reasonably determine for the conduct of the Company's business.

Member Meetings

21. A meeting may be called by any Member providing that

reasonable notice has been given to the other Members.

22. Regular meetings of the Members will be held annually.

Voting

23. Each Member will be entitled to cast votes on any matter based upon the proportion of that Member's Capital Contributions in the Company.

Admission of New Members

24. A new Member may only be admitted to the Company with a unanimous vote of the existing Members.

25. The new Member agrees to be bound by all the covenants, terms, and conditions of this Agreement, inclusive of all current and future amendments. Further, a new Member will execute such documents as are needed to affect the admission of the new Member. Any new Member will receive such business interest in the Company as determined by a unanimous decision of the other Members.

Voluntary Withdrawal of a Member

26. A Member may not withdraw from the Company without the unanimous consent of the remaining Members. Any such unauthorized withdrawal will be considered a wrongful dissociation and a breach of this Agreement. In the event of any such wrongful dissociation, the withdrawing Member will be liable to the remaining Members for any damages incurred by the remaining Members including but not limited to the loss of future earnings.

27. The voluntary withdrawal of a Member will have no effect upon the continuance of the Company.

28. It remains incumbent on the withdrawing Member to exercise this dissociation in good faith and to minimize any present or future harm done to the remaining Members as a result of the withdrawal.

Involuntary Withdrawal of a Member

29. Events leading to the involuntary withdrawal of a Member from the Company will include but not be limited to: death of a Member; Member mental incapacity; Member disability preventing reasonable participation in the Company; Member incompetence; breach of fiduciary duties by a Member; criminal conviction of a Member; Operation of Law against a Member or a legal judgment against a Member that can reasonably be expected to bring the business or societal reputation of the Company into disrepute. Expulsion of a Member can also occur on application by the Company or another Member, where it has been judicially determined that the Member: has engaged in wrongful conduct that adversely and materially affected the Company's business; has willfully or persistently committed a material breach of this Agreement or of a duty owed to the Company or to the other Members; or has engaged in conduct relating to the Company's business that makes it not reasonably practicable to carry on the business with the Member.

30. The involuntary withdrawal of a Member will have no effect upon the continuance of the Company.

Dissociation of a Member

31. In the event of either a voluntary or involuntary withdrawal of a Member, if the remaining Members elect to purchase the interest of the withdrawing Member, the remaining Members will serve written notice of such election, including the purchase price and method and schedule of payment for the withdrawing Member's Interests, upon the withdrawing Member, their executor, administrator, trustee, committee or analogous fiduciary within a reasonable period after acquiring knowledge of the change in circumstance to the affected Member. The purchase amount of any buyout of a Member's Interests will be determined as set out in the Valuation of Interest section of this Agreement.

32. Valuation and distribution will be determined as described in the Valuation of Interest section of this Agreement.

33. The remaining Members retain the right to seek damages from a dissociated Member where the dissociation resulted from a malicious or criminal act by the dissociated Member or where the dissociated Member had breached their fiduciary duty to the Company or was in breach of this Agreement or had acted in a way that could reasonably be foreseen to bring harm or damage to the Company or to the reputation of the Company.

34. A dissociated Member will only have liability for Company obligations that were incurred during their time as a Member. On dissociation of a Member, the Company will prepare, file, serve, and publish all notices required by law to protect the dissociated Member from liability for future Company obligations.

35. Where the remaining Members have purchased the interest of a dissociated Member, the purchase amount will be paid in full, but without interest, within 90 days of the date of withdrawal. The Company will retain exclusive rights to use of the trade name and firm name and all related brand and model names of the Company.

Right of First Purchase

36. In the event that a Member's Interest in the Company is or will be sold, due to any reason, the remaining Members will have a right of first purchase of that Member's Interest. The value of that interest in the Company will be the lower of the value set out in the Valuation of Interest section of this Agreement and any third party offer that the Member wishes to accept.

Assignment of Interest

37. A Member's financial interest in the Company can only be assigned to another Member and cannot be assigned to a third party except with the unanimous consent of the remaining Members.

38. In the event that a Member's interest in the company is transferred or assigned as the result of a court order or Operation of Law, the trustee in bankruptcy or other person acquiring that Member's Interests in the Company will only acquire that Member's economic rights and interests and will not acquire any other rights of that Member or be admitted as a Member of the Company or have the right to exercise any management or voting interests.

Valuation of Interest

39. In the event of a dissociation or the dissolution of the Company, each Member's financial interest in the Company will be in proportion to the following schedule:

Member	Dissolution Distribution Percent
John Doe	51%
Jones Family Trust	49%

40. In the absence of a written agreement setting a value, the value of the Company will be based on the fair market value appraisal of all Company assets (less liabilities) determined in accordance with generally accepted accounting principles (GAAP). This appraisal will be conducted by an independent accounting firm agreed to by all Members. An appraiser will be appointed within a reasonable period of the date of withdrawal or dissolution. The results of the appraisal will be binding on all Members. The intent of this section is to ensure the survival of the Company despite the withdrawal of any individual Member.

41. No allowance will be made for goodwill, trade name, patents, or other intangible assets, except where those assets have been reflected on the Company books immediately prior to valuation.

Dissolution

42. The Company may be dissolved by a unanimous vote of the Members. The Company will also be dissolved on the occurrence of events specified in the Act.

43. Upon Dissolution of the Company and liquidation of
     Company property, and after payment of all selling costs
     and expenses, the liquidator will distribute the Company
     assets to the following groups according to the following
     order of priority:

     a. in satisfaction of liabilities to Creditors except Company
         obligations to current Members;

     b. in satisfaction of Company debt obligations to current
         Members; and then

     c. to the Members based on Member financial interest, as
         set out in the Valuation of Interest section of this
         Agreement.

Records

44. The Company will at all times maintain accurate records of
     the following:

     a. Information regarding the status of the business and the
         financial condition of the Company.

     b. A copy of the Company federal, state, and local income
         taxes for each year, promptly after becoming available.

     c. Name and last known business, residential, or mailing
         address of each Member, as well as the date that person
         became a Member.

     d. A copy of this Agreement and any articles or certificate
         of formation, as well as all amendments, together with
         any executed copies of any written powers of attorney
         pursuant to which this Agreement, articles or certificate,
         and any amendments have been executed.

     e. The cash, property, and services contributed to the

Company by each Member, along with a description and value, and any contributions that have been agreed to be made in the future.

45. Each Member has the right to demand, within a reasonable period of time, a copy of any of the above documents for any purpose reasonably related to their interest as a Member of the Company, at their expense.

Books of Account

46. Accurate and complete books of account of the transactions of the Company will be kept in accordance with generally accepted accounting principles (GAAP) and at all reasonable times will be available and open to inspection and examination by any Member. The books and records of the Company will reflect all the Company's transactions and will be appropriate and adequate for the business conducted by the Company.

Banking and Company Funds

47. The funds of the Company will be placed in such investments and banking accounts as will be designated by the Members. All withdrawals from these accounts will be made by the duly authorized agent or agents of the Company as appointed by unanimous consent of the Members. Company funds will be held in the name of the Company and will not be commingled with those of any other person or entity.

Audit

48. Any of the Members will have the right to request an audit

of the Company books. The cost of the audit will be borne by the Company. The audit will be performed by an accounting firm acceptable to all the Members. Not more than one (1) audit will be required by any or all of the Members for any fiscal year.

Tax Treatment

49. This Company is intended to be treated as a Partnership, for the purposes of Federal and State Income Tax.

Partnership Representative

50. John Doe will be the Partnership representative ("the Partnership Representative") with the sole authority to act on behalf of the Company in relation to IRS tax audits pursuant to Chapter 63 Subchapter C of the Internal Revenue Code of 1986.

51. The Partnership Representative is appointed for the current tax year and subsequent tax years until otherwise designated by the Members.

52. The Members will indemnify the Partnership Representative from and against all claims, actions, suits, demands, damages, obligations, losses, settlements, judgments, costs, and expenses brought by the Members or any of them in relation to any acts or omissions in the conduct of the role of Partnership Representative provided that the Partnership Representative is a Member, except to the extent that such losses result from, in whole or in part, the negligence, willful misconduct or unlawful action of the Partnership Representative.

53. The Partnership Representative will promptly advise the Members of any audit of the Company initiated by the IRS and provide regular updates to the Members on the progress of such audits and any resulting settlement negotiations. The Partnership Representative will be generally accountable to the Members and will obtain the majority approval of the Members for (i) any decisions affecting the tax liability of the Company or the Members; and (ii) any decision finalizing tax settlement with the IRS.

54. The Partnership Representative may resign from the position by serving notice in writing on both the Company and the IRS. The Company, acting by majority vote, may revoke the designation of the Partnership Representative by serving notice on the Partnership Representative and the IRS and simultaneously appointing a new Partnership Representative for that taxable year.

55. Whether serving in an active capacity or not, any person who has served as Partnership Representative in respect of any given taxable year or portion thereof will remain accountable to the Company, throughout the period of limitation relating to that taxable year, in respect of any notification received from the IRS and will promptly advise the Company of any and all such correspondence.

56. In the event that a tax settlement reached between the IRS and the Partnership Representative is not satisfactory to one or more of the Members and the matter cannot be resolved through negotiation in good faith at a meeting of the Members, then, two weeks, or such longer period as the Members may agree, following such meeting the Members

agree to submit the dispute to mediation.

Annual Report

57. As soon as practicable after the close of each fiscal year, the Company will furnish to each Member an annual report showing a full and complete account of the condition of the Company including all information as will be necessary for the preparation of each Member's income or other tax returns. This report will consist of at least:

    a. A copy of the Company's federal income tax returns for that fiscal year.

    b. Balance sheet.

    c. A breakdown of the profit and loss attributable to each Member.

Goodwill

58. The goodwill of the Company will be assessed at an amount to be determined by appraisal using generally accepted accounting principles (GAAP).

Governing Law

59. The Members submit to the jurisdiction of the courts of the State of New Hampshire for the enforcement of this Agreement or any arbitration award or decision arising from this Agreement.

Force Majeure

60. A Member will be free of liability to the Company where the Member is prevented from executing their obligations under this Agreement in whole or in part due to force majeure, such as earthquake, typhoon, flood, fire, and war

or any other unforeseen and uncontrollable event where the Member has communicated the circumstance of the event to any and all other Members and where the Member has taken any and all appropriate action to satisfy his duties and obligations to the Company and to mitigate the effects of the event.

Forbidden Acts

61. No Member may do any act in contravention of this Agreement.

62. No Member may permit, intentionally or unintentionally, the assignment of express, implied, or apparent authority to a third party that is not a Member of the Company.

63. No Member may do any act that would make it impossible to carry on the ordinary business of the Company.

64. No Member will have the right or authority to bind or obligate the Company to any extent with regard to any matter outside the intended purpose of the Company.

65. No Member may confess a judgment against the Company.

66. Any violation of the above forbidden acts will be deemed an Involuntary Withdrawal and may be treated accordingly by the remaining Members.

Indemnification

67. All Members will be indemnified and held harmless by the Company from and against any and all claims of any nature, whatsoever, arising out of a Member's participation in Company affairs. A Member will not be entitled to

indemnification under this section for liability arising out of gross negligence or willful misconduct of the Member or the breach by the Member of any provisions of this Agreement.

Liability

68. A Member or any employee will not be liable to the Company or to any other Member for any mistake or error in judgment or for any act or omission believed in good faith to be within the scope of authority conferred or implied by this Agreement or the Company. The Member or employee will be liable only for any and all acts and omissions involving intentional wrongdoing.

Liability Insurance

69. The Company may acquire insurance on behalf of any Member, employee, agent, or other person engaged in the business interest of the Company against any liability asserted against them or incurred by them while acting in good faith on behalf of the Company.

Life Insurance

70. The Company will have the right to acquire life insurance on the lives of any or all of the Members, whenever it is deemed necessary by the Company. Each Member will cooperate fully with the Company in obtaining any such policies of life insurance.

Amendment of This Agreement

71. No amendment or modification of this Agreement will be valid or effective unless in writing and signed by all Members.

Title to Company Property

72. Title to all Company property will remain in the name of the Company. No Member or group of Members will have any ownership interest in Company property in whole or in part.

Miscellaneous

73. Time is of the essence in this Agreement.

74. This Agreement may be executed in counterparts.

75. Headings are inserted for the convenience of the Members only and are not to be considered when interpreting this Agreement. Words in the singular mean and include the plural and vice versa. Words in the masculine gender include the feminine gender and vice versa. Words in a neutral gender include the masculine gender and the feminine gender and vice versa.

76. If any term, covenant, condition, or provision of this Agreement is held by a court of competent jurisdiction to be invalid, void, or unenforceable, it is the Members' intent that such provision be reduced in scope by the court only to the extent deemed necessary by that court to render the provision reasonable and enforceable, and the remainder of the provisions of this Agreement will in no way be affected, impaired, or invalidated as a result.

77. This Agreement contains the entire agreement between the Members. All negotiations and understandings have been included in this Agreement. Statements or representations that may have been made by any Member during the

negotiation stages of this Agreement may in some way be inconsistent with this final written Agreement. All such statements have no force or effect in respect to this Agreement. Only the written terms of this Agreement will bind the Members.

78. This Agreement and the terms and conditions contained in this Agreement apply to and are binding upon each Member's successors, assigns, executors, administrators, beneficiaries, and representatives.

79. Any notices or delivery required here will be deemed completed when hand-delivered, delivered by agent, or seven (7) days after being placed in the post, postage prepaid, to the Members at the addresses contained in this Agreement or as the Members may later designate in writing.

80. All of the rights, remedies, and benefits provided by this Agreement will be cumulative and will not be exclusive of any other such rights, remedies, and benefits allowed by law.

Definitions

81. For the purpose of this Agreement, the following terms are defined as follows:

    a. "Additional Contribution" means Capital Contributions, other than Initial Contributions, made by Members to the Company.

    b. "Capital Contribution" means the total amount of cash, property, or services contributed to the Company by any one Member.

c. "Distributions" means a payment of Company profits to the Members.

d. "Initial Contribution" means the initial Capital Contributions made by any Member to acquire an interest in the Company.

e. "Member's Interests" means the Member's collective rights, including but not limited to, the Member's right to share in profits, Member's right to a share of Company assets on dissolution of the Company, Member's voting rights, and Member's rights to participate in the management of the Company.

f. "Net Profits or Losses" means the net profits or losses of the Company as determined by generally accepted accounting principles (GAAP).

g. "Operation of Law" means rights or duties that are cast upon a party by the law, without any act or agreement on the part of the individual, including, but not limited to, an assignment for the benefit of Creditors, a divorce, or a bankruptcy.

h. "Principal Office" means the office whether inside or outside the State of New Hampshire where the executive or management of the Company maintain their primary office.

i. "Voting Members" means the Members who belong to a membership class that has voting power. Where there is only one class of Members, then those Members constitute the Voting Members.

IN WITNESS WHEREOF the Members have duly affixed their signatures under hand and seal on this _____ day of _____, _____.

_____

Managing Member

_____

Member

Independent Contractor Agreement:

<u>**Independent Contractor's Agreement**</u>
<u>*with*</u>
<u>**Acme Construction Company, Inc.**</u>

This Agreement is made _____,_____, 20____ by and between Acme Construction Company, Inc. a Massachusetts Corporation, hereinafter the "Company" and _____ _____, an Individual, at _____, Massachusetts the Independent Contractor. The purpose of this agreement is to clearly define the Independent Contractor relationship and Contractual Agreement between the parties identified above and to absolutely dis-affirm any employer/employee relationship.

This Contract entered into by the above parties expressly recognizes as its basis the Constitution of the united States of America and the above mentioned states of the Union as well as American Common Law. We freely enter into this Independent Contractor Contract with each other unrestricted by any acts, statutes, ordinances, regulations, or customs not in conformity with a private citizen's rights, privileges, and immunities secured or protected by this nation's founding documents.

This Agreement is subject to and is in consideration of the following conditions, promises, and understandings by and between the Company and the Independent Contractor to which we do agree:

A. Services

Contractor agrees to provide services and perform these services in order to achieve the mutually desired results as agreed to herein:

1. To provide carpentry and other skills necessary to perform certain work on an independent basis as required by the Company from time to time;

2. To include but not limited to constructing porches and other structures, remodeling, and making additions as well as other jobs of the trade.

B. Compensation for Services

Acme Construction Company, Inc. agrees to provide adequate compensation to the Contractor for these services recognizing that without them the position of the Company would be weakened. Compensation shall be paid at a rate of $_____.00 per hour or as otherwise agreed upon at the start of each individual job, engagement, or assignment. It is agreed that aforesaid compensation shall not be diminished by deductions of any kind by the Company and it shall be the Contractor's sole responsibility to pay lawfully required taxes.

C. Results

The Company retains the exclusive right to approve or disapprove of the Contractor's services.

D. Equipment and Materials

The Company agrees to supply the necessary equipment and materials whether by providing them to the Contractor or by agreement to reimburse approved costs.

E. Length of Contract

The period of this agreement shall continue from month-to-month or until the Contractor's services are completed. The Contractor may start and cease work at will as long as services are satisfactory to the Company and no supervision of Contractor shall be deemed necessary by the Company in the details of services performed after an initial introduction to the needs and requirements of the Company and/or its customer.

F. Nonexclusive Services

In providing the Services under this Agreement it is expressly agreed that the Contractor is acting as an independent contractor and not as an employee. The Contractor is serving as a free agent and independent contractor holding himself out to other clients as such for work or contracts as he/she sees fit to do. The Contractor and the Company acknowledge that this Agreement does not create a Partnership or joint venture between them and is exclusively a contract for service. The Company is not required to pay, or make any contributions to, any social security; local, state, or federal tax; unemployment compensation; workers' compensation; insurance premium; or profit-sharing, pension, or any other employee benefit for the

Contractor during the Term. The Contractor is responsible for paying, and complying with reporting requirements for, all local, state, and federal taxes related to payments made to the Contractor under this Agreement. The Contractor may start and cease work at will as long as services are satisfactory to the Company and no supervision of Contractor shall be deemed necessary by the Company in the details of services performed after an initial introduction to the needs and requirements of the Company and/or its customer.

In Witness Whereof, Acme Construction Company, Inc. and Contractor execute this Contract on_____, 20____ at _____, Massachusetts.

_____

Tom Jones, President

_____

Independent Contractor

Sample Power-of-Attorney:

GENERAL POWER OF ATTORNEY
(Durable)

KNOW ALL MEN BY THESE PRESENTS, that I, _____, the

undersigned Principle residing at _____,

grant a general power of attorney to _____ residing at

_____, and appoint said individual as my

attorney-in-fact to act in my name, place and stead in any way which I myself could do

if I were personally present, including but not limited to the following:

a. To ask, demand, receive, sue for and recover all sums of money and any and all other property, tangible or intangible, due or hereafter becoming due and owing, or belonging to me, and to make, give and execute, receipts, releases, satisfactions, or other discharges therefor.

b. To make, execute, endorse, accept, and deliver in my name or in the name of my attorney-in-fact all checks, notes, drafts and all other instruments, of whatsoever nature, as to my said attorney-in-fact may deem necessary to conserve my interests and/or exercise the rights and powers granted herein.

c. To execute, acknowledge and deliver any and all contracts, deeds, leases, and any other agreement or document affecting any and all property now owned by me or hereafter acquired.

d. To enter into and take possession of any real estate belonging to me, the possession of which I may be or may become entitled, and to receive in my name and to my use any rents and profits belonging to me, and to lease such real estate in such manner that my attorney-in-fact shall deem necessary and proper, and from time to time to renew leases.

e. To commence, prosecute, compromise, settle, adjust and/or discontinue any claims, suits, actions or legal proceedings for the recovery of sums of money or property now or hereafter due or to become due, or held by or belonging to me.

f. To prepare, or cause to be prepared all tax returns, of which the law makes me liable or a person liable to file or to pay; to execute and file tax returns in my name and on my behalf; and to settle tax disputes.

g. To take any actions necessary and proper to carry on, conduct and manage my business affairs, and to engage in and transact any lawful business in my name and on my behalf.

h. To defend, all actions and suits which shall be commended against me, and to compromise, settle, and adjust all actions, accounts, dues, and demands in such manner as my said attorney-in-fact shall deem appropriate.

i. To do and perform every act and thing necessary or proper in the exercise of the rights and powers herein granted, as fully as I might or could do if personally present, with full power of substitution or revocation, hereby ratifying and confirming all that my attorney-in-fact, or his substitute or substitutes, shall lawfully do or cause to be done by virtue of the authority granted herein.

1. **Interpretation.** This instrument is to be construed and interpreted as a general power of attorney. The enumeration of specific items, acts, rights, or powers herein does not limit or restrict, and is not to be construed or interpreted as limiting or restricting the general powers herein granted to my attorney-in-fact.

2. **Durable Nature of Power of Attorney.** This power of attorney shall not be affected by my subsequent disability, incapacity or incompetence.

3. **Requirements For Revocation of Power of Attorney.** I may revoke this power of attorney by giving written notice to the attorney-in-fact. However, such revocation shall not be effective as to a third party who relies in good faith upon this power of attorney unless such third party has actual or constructive knowledge of the revocation or the revocation has been recorded in the public records where I reside.

4. **Acceptance of Attorney-In-Fact Appointment.** By signing this document, my attorney-in-fact accepts the appointment as my attorney-in-fact.

WHEREFORE, the following parties sign this instrument on this _____ day of _____, 20___.

_____   _____
Witness   , Principle

_____   _____
Witness   , Attorney-In-Fact

STATE OF _____)
)ss
COUNTY OF _____)

On this _____ day of _____, 20___ before me, a Notary Public in and for the State of _____, personally appeared the above signatories, known or shown to me to be the persons whose names are subscribed to the foregoing instrument, and acknowledged to me that they executed the same as their free act and deed.

_____   My Commission Expires: _____
Notary Public

APPENDIX D

Payment Option & Credit Sheets

Below are examples of a Credit Sheet and a Payments Option Sheet you should have ready to go when dealing with Creditors and Vendors.

Your Company Name
123 S. Main St., Suite 2
City, State 12345
Email: Cme@yourcompany.com
800-123-4567

Your Company Name References

Contact Person: Your Name, Title

Federal Tax ID: 12-34567890

Bank: Local FED Bank
456 Main Street
City, State 12345
TEL: 800-987-6543

References: Joe's Stationary Store
34 Front Street
Plainville, OH 02762
Contact: Joe Miller
TEL: 800-345-0987

Rental Services
24 Town Road
PO Box 9
Smallville, MA 01567
Contact: Jack Smith
TEL: 888-991-4567

Local Supply House
23 Depot Street
Bigville, CA 97532
Contact: Frank Johnson
TEL: 213-478-8666

West Coast Division address:
Your Company Name
98 Town Road
Town, XX 01569
213-556-9922
Email: Jmiller@yourcompany.com

Payment Options and Instructions

Physical Address:

Acme Enterprises
83 Middle Road
Anytown, MA 01910

Wiring Instructions:

Wire funds to: Sovereign Bank
369 Main Street
Wakefield, MA 01880

ABA (routing #): 011075150   Swift Code: SVRNUS65

For Credit to: Acme Enterprises
Account #: 73504969243

Credit Card Payment:

Type:_ Visa _ M/C

Name on Card: _____

Card #: _____

Exp. Date: _____

Billing Address of Card: _____

_____

Total Amount to Charge: $_____ (US)

Applications for 30 day net open accounts available on request.
If application for credit is not made in advance of order the order may be delayed by approval procedure.

Acme Enterprises Telephone 888 600-6100, Fax 508-312-8665 or Email Orders@Acme.com

About the Author

A Massachusetts native, Scott Dion has been a business owner and entrepreneur since 1986. After apprenticing as a Machinist and eventually becoming the owner of a Machine Company, he went on to study Real Estate and Business Law. He has been a Licensed Insurance Agent, Investment Broker, and Commodity Trader. Scott's interest in accounting and tax law led to his partnering in the ownership of multiple businesses and an invitation to serve on the boards of many others, from Machining, Landscape, Construction, and Employment Companies to Doctors' Offices, Consulting Firms, and Trucking Companies. As a Business and Estate Planner specializing in Trusts, Scott is more than qualified to offer his expertise to the reader.

Everything Business, LLC
36 Center St. # 172
Wolfeboro, NH 03894
603-651-0220
Support@EverythingBusinessLLC.com
www.EverythingBusinessLLC.com

Specializing in:

- Business Formation
- Trusts
- Bookkeeping Access to your Company files via Virtual Desktop connections for you and your employees on Cloud Computing System.

Initial appointment (by phone or in-person) for Business or Estate Planning is always free of charge. (*Company is affiliated with the Author.*)

****

Special Offer: (*Proof of Purchase Required*)

Turn-Key Business Formation (*Includes all of the following*):

- ✓ Registration of any Corporation, LLC, or Partnership in any State
- ✓ Operating Agreement, Minutes, and Bylaws appropriate for Entity chosen
- ✓ Domain Name and Landing Page on the Internet as close a fit to your chosen name as possible

- ✓ One-year access to Virtual Desktop hosting QuickBooks for your Company bookkeeping, along with a host of other software available for use from any device anywhere
- ✓ One year of an email account matching your domain name with multiple alias email names available for use
- ✓ One-year Resident Agent Service if your Company is not in your State of residence.
- ✓ Submission of Application for EIN with IRS.gov
- ✓ Five hours of Consulting and/or Training for you or your employee in bookkeeping, business management, or the topic(s) of your choice
- ✓ Stockholder or Family Trust formed to hold business interest or as a container for future use

Even as a do-it-yourself endeavor, starting a business with this check list would cost you, conservatively, $2,800. Done by a local attorney or accountant, it would more than likely exceed $5,000—if they would even provide you with the entire list of services. At Everything Business, LLC, purchasing these as separate services would run $3,500. A $2,500 package deal on their website is being offered here to the reader for $1,995, far less than it would cost to do it yourself.